Fred Crix

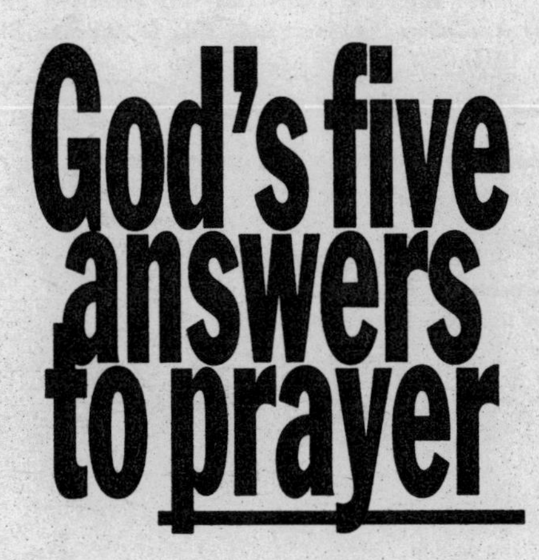

CROSSWAY BOOKS

CROSSWAY BOOKS
38 De Montfort Street, Leicester LE1 7GP, England

First published 1999

British Library Cataloguing in Publication Data
A catalogue record for this book is available from the British Library.

ISBN 1–85684–182–8

Set in Garamond
Typeset and printed in Great Britain

To the Melrose housegroup,
Milton Keynes,
with whom I have spent many
enriching hours in prayer

Contents

Notes

Biblical references

There are many references throughout this book to people and situations in the Bible. For easier reading, some of these references are not given in the text; if you need to look them up, you will find them in Appendix 1. The version used is the Good News Bible.

Acknowledgments

There are five people whose help, encouragement and constructive criticism have made a real contribution to this book. They are the Rev. Glyn Carter, the Rev. and Mrs Roy Cave, David Page and Hilary Brand; my warmest thanks to all of them. I am also indebted to the Rev. Lindesay Godfrey's book, *More About Prayer*, for the account of the trapped miners mentioned in the Preface.

Preface

There were once three miners, Tom, Harry and Fred, who were trapped below ground by a fall of rock. As time passed, and the possibility of rescue began to seem more remote, Tom suggested that one of them should pray. At first, they all decided that they wouldn't know what to say, so they dropped the idea. As time slowly passed and no help came, they realized the situation was desperate. They decided that prayer was their last hope.

So, after a long pause while he worked out what to say, Harry prayed, 'Lord, tha knaws I've never troubled thee in't past, and if tha gets us out o' this mess, I promise I'll never trouble thee again.' And they all said, 'Amen.'

They must have got out or we wouldn't know about the prayer (yes, it really happened), but I wonder what happened after the rescue. Did they believe some miraculous action by God had saved them? If they did, how did they show their gratitude? Or did they decide they would have been saved anyway? That it was either luck or the rescue service, but not God? And did they then forget all about God until they faced another crisis?

There are many people in this world for whom prayer is like that. They acknowledge that there is an almighty power 'up there somewhere', but they really believe that they can ignore him until they need something.

I hope committed Christians understand God a lot better than that. But I believe that many thousands of church-going Christians still make little effort to contact God frequently and personally. Even those who do, often doubt whether it makes any real difference. Even those who *do* believe it makes a difference may have great difficulty in reaching that point where they feel they have 'got through' to God – where their hearts have been lifted above the mundane into the spiritual.

If you are one of those who are able to establish contact with God whenever you wish, if you always find prayer a joy and a never-failing source of guidance and inner strength, then read no further. Instead, just tell me your secret!

If, however, you have to admit that occasionally (or perhaps often) prayer is more duty than pleasure, and you heartily wish that you found it more natural and helpful than you do now, this book is for you. It is written by one who believes in prayer and derives much help from it, but who still finds that it can be difficult and is constantly meeting others who do too.

It is a practical workbook for ordinary Christians, not an academic treatise. You will find plenty of illustrations from the Bible, and others from day-to-day life in which you may recognize yourself!

Fred Crix

Chapter 1

What prayer is ... and what it isn't

Before discussing any subject, it is usually a good idea to be clear about what it is. So let us try to define prayer. It has been described as having a conversation with God. That definition has the merit of reminding us that prayer should be a dialogue, with both God and us having things to say and things to hear. But in other ways it won't do. It puts too much emphasis on words and how they are spoken, and fails to explain adequately how we 'hear' what God is saying to us.

It's better to regard prayer as *opening our thoughts to God and asking him to replace them with his.* That is not easy to take in at first reading; it needs to be thought about for a while. Certainly it is radically different from the way many of us pray, whether in church or at home. We often associate prayer, except in emergencies, with certain postures and a special phraseology. It's like straightening our tie or seeing our hair is in place before we go into the boss's office. We fail to realize that since God reads our *thoughts*, he will be listening to us before we have even decided what to say.

We share with God our feelings of joy or sadness, satisfaction or fear, our hopes, our needs, our doubts, our uncertainties – everything. In doing so, we are asking – and should be expecting – the Holy Spirit to go into action. (The Holy Spirit is God at work within and around us.)

The action may take different forms. We may find our hearts being filled there and then with a feeling of deep peace or radiant joy. It happens. By contrast, we may experience a feeling of God-given discontent. That will indicate that there is some action *we* need to take – an apology to someone we've hurt, a visit to someone who's lonely, or perhaps a complete change of direction in our lives. If that happens, we'll never find real peace until we have obeyed. But when we have, it's wonderful.

Then again, we may not feel anything at the time; but in the ensuing days or weeks, we find our views have changed. We may have a feeling of warmth towards someone we previously had little time for. We may have an assurance on some aspect of our faith that had previously baffled us.

All these experiences are God working in us, answering our prayers. Very often, we do not connect the answers to the prayers until we look back later on. Then we realize how often we get it wrong, how patient our heavenly Father is with us, how his wisdom guides us and his power protects us.

You'll notice I've been following the usual practice

of describing God as 'he' or 'Father'. If you are a feminist, it may have made your hackles rise. So let's address this question of gender before we go any further. God is not Superman – he is the Almighty Creator Spirit. Because he is not physical, we cannot think of him as having a body and arms and legs. Indeed, he cannot really be described in human terms at all because he is so far above the understanding of our mortal minds.

But we *can* think of him as personal because he has all the human attributes of knowing, loving and caring. He displays all that is best in fatherhood and motherhood. So he is *neither* male nor female but he is *both* masculine and feminine. Why then, do we always say 'he'? For two reasons.

First, because when humankind dimly began to be aware of God at all, what is now called male chauvinism was the accepted way of thinking, by women as well as men. It wasn't seen as an attempt to subjugate women; it was just the natural order of things, and it is only in the last few decades that the principle has been seriously challenged.

Secondly, because our language doesn't have pronouns that are neuter but still personal. To describe God as 'it' would appear most irreverent; to describe him as 'he and she' would be dreadfully clumsy. In any case, masculine personal pronouns have traditionally been used to include both genders. These days, we try to avoid using 'men' when we really mean 'people', but it is still common to allow 'he' to include 'she', as when we speak of *man*kind.

So 'he' it is – but never take that as meaning that

God is 'the Old Man in the sky'. He is much greater than that.

Because of our earthbound way of thinking, in which a message given earnestly enough or often enough is bound to influence the hearer, we find it difficult to accept that prayer is meant to change *us*, not God. Catherine Marshall wrote, 'God insists that we ask, not because *he* needs to know our situation, but because *we* need the spiritual discipline of asking.' Of course he knows; he knew before we did.

It was George Meredith who wrote, 'Who rises from his prayer a better man, his prayer is answered.' That reminds us that God never changes, because he doesn't need to. We do, constantly. This is where we often get confused between seeing God as the great Creator and a loving Father. We find it hard to accept that God can actually know each of us by name, can love us – even when we rebel against him – and always want the best for us. But he can and does.

If you hadn't thought about that before, you'll need a while to take it in. Just think about it. God, the architect of the whole universe, giver and sustainer of all life, all-knowing, all-powerful, Lord of time and eternity, space and infinity, will actually enter our mortal minds to guide, to enable, to heal and to bless. Not a messenger, but God himself, for he and his Spirit are one. Prayer is the way of inviting him in – the only way.

When we think of God in all his power and glory, we realize that he is beyond the understanding of our earthly minds, and therefore we cannot think of him changing. Nor does he change, but he does *respond*. If he didn't, there would be no point in our praying. So prayer can have a great effect on us, but can our prayers really affect other people? Yes, they can. Just as we open our hearts to God and ask him, by the Holy Spirit, to control our thoughts and actions, so we can ask that he will work in others too. Our prayers for others (I've heard them described, simply but beautifully, as loving thoughts) can release spiritual power into their lives just as they can in ours.

Just how that spiritual activity operates is likely to remain far beyond our understanding, but that doesn't matter. All we need to remember is that prayer, so long as we remember that it is not our wishes but God's purposes that are sovereign, is a way of getting involved in the universal and powerful activity of the Holy Spirit.

When we pray to him as our Father, we can be assured that he really is moved by our prayers. In *The Widow in the Bye Street*, John Masefield gives us a lovely picture of God when he writes, 'God warms his hands at man's heart when he prays.' But the fact that God delights in the prayers of his children must not mislead us into seeing God as all-indulgent rather than all-wise, and end up submitting our requests when we should be submitting ourselves.

Prayer then, is a *spiritual* exercise, with our spirit making contact with God's Spirit. It is not subject to the earthly rules of communication which cannot operate without sight or sound. It's true that our minds are involved (because we need to think) and so are our hearts (because love is being expressed), but prayer that *only* operates on the human level is not really prayer at all. It only becomes prayer when the gap between our material world and God's eternal world is bridged. When that does happen, great power can be released, as when a high-voltage current jumps between two electrodes.

That is not to say that the effect is always dramatic. God is all-powerful, but he does not always answer our prayers with a voice from heaven or some other shattering experience. Very rarely, in fact. God's 'still small voice' can be just as effective as a mighty wind, an earthquake or a fire if he so chooses, as Elijah discovered when he fled to Mount Sinai to escape the threats of Queen Jezebel. Note those words 'if he chooses'. God may respond to prayer with some vision that reveals aspects of his truth or glory, or the pray-er may find himself or herself using ecstatic language (the spiritual gift described in the Bible as tongues), or perhaps, like John Wesley when he had a conversion experience in Aldersgate in 1738, he may feel his 'heart strangely warmed' or just become aware of a sense of deep peace.

God deals with us in different ways because he knows we have different personalities and therefore different needs. Some Christians are volatile by nature, and their spiritual lives will always be a succession of 'highs and lows'. Sometimes they will be filled with joy and enthusiasm while at other times they will be dispirited and asking others to pray for them. Others display a much steadier spiritual life. They show little emotion but their actions are guided by a quiet faith.

We sometimes hear the expression 'praying in the Spirit', as though that is somehow different from 'ordinary' prayer, but that cannot be so, because there is no prayer without the Spirit. (Where the term is used to imply 'praying in tongues', that is another matter. That is a feature of charismatic worship.)

It is possible to frame prayers in beautiful language, or read ones that others have prepared (whether recently or in the distant past) and repeat them all day and all night without ever making any real contact with God. Such prayers may still be uplifting, in the same way that reading a good book or listening to a Beethoven symphony may be, but they can leave our minds as earthbound as when we began, unless we are consciously using them as a means for our spirits to reach out to God.

It is equally possible to chat away to God giving no more serious thought to what we are saying than if we were talking to the cat. That too is not real prayer.

We need to take prayer seriously and be disciplined about it, but at the same time remember that we can be completely natural. There is a hymn by John Burton, who was a Sunday-school teacher in London's East End for twenty-seven years, which reminds us that when we pray, we need to give God our full attention:

> I often say my prayers,
> But do I ever pray?
> And do the wishes of my heart
> Go with the words I say?
>
> I may as well kneel down
> And worship gods of stone,
> As offer to the living God
> A prayer of words alone.

For words without the heart
  The Lord will never hear;
Nor will he to those lips attend
  Whose prayers are not sincere.

Lord, teach me what I need,
  And teach me how to pray;
And do not let me seek thy grace,
  Not meaning what I say.

That is from *Hymns of Faith*, in the section headed 'For young children'. I'm not sure that's where it should be, because however simple the language, the thought is profound.

Now let's get practical.

A typical prayer meeting

Have you ever been to a prayer meeting like this?

> After one or two hymns, the leader asks for items for prayer. Someone asks for prayer for old Mrs Hodges who has just had a fall and broken her hip. Another says they should pray for the minister, and that prompts a prayer request for Helen, a missionary in Brazil. Harold asks for a prayer for guidance because he thinks he is being called to full-time Christian service but doesn't know where.
>
> Derek has just been made redundant, and Ruth's son, Wayne, has a job interview the next day. Sylvia is taking her driving test in a few days time; would they pray especially hard, because

it's her fourth test and she is not very confident.

Mary keeps getting migraines and is sure she is under attack by Satan. Fiona is about to take nine GCSEs and her mother, Linda, wants prayer that she might do well. George says they should pray for the government; and Ken, who supports the opposition party, narrows his eyes momentarily. Jean has a colleague whose uncle has just had a heart attack; no, she doesn't know how bad it was or what his name is. Rachel says they should pray for Africa but doesn't say why and nobody asks.

Pat wants prayer for revival, and would they keep praying for Henry who has been unwell for a long time and doesn't seem to be getting any better. Sue asks everyone to pray for fine weather on the day of the junior-church anniversary because there is to be a picnic in the afternoon. Stella reports that her husband, Ron, is flying to the States on business and would they pray for 'journeying mercies'.

I'm sure many of you will have recognized that account. Change the names and it could probably have happened in your church or housegroup.

Let me make it clear that I am not for one moment trying to ridicule that prayer meeting. In fact, that scenario has some very good points – very good indeed. First, there's the fact that it is happening at all; too often it doesn't. Yet here they are, a group of Christians who have come together to share their concerns with each other and with God. What's more, they probably meet regularly, which means that they are taking their praying seriously.

Secondly, there is an obvious sense of caring for one another. They see themselves as part of a family, in which each member has a responsibility towards all the others.

Thirdly, their interests are not confined to themselves and their activities. Their minds are open to what is happening beyond their own circle; they care about what is happening on the mission field and in world affairs.

Fourthly, this group clearly have a firm belief in God's power to achieve what they ask. In other words, they want that prayer meeting to be what the Baptist preacher, C. H. Spurgeon, called 'the throbbing machinery of the church'.

Yet it raises some important questions about what they expect to happen as a result of their praying.

Take Mrs Hodges, for example. Are they asking – and expecting – that her fractured femur will be more expertly set, or heal more quickly, than if they hadn't prayed? Is Mary's prayer request really directed to God or is it addressed to him but really meant for others in the group? That is, is it just a cry for help and encouragement?

And where was the penitence, the thanksgiving, the worship, and the pleas for spiritual guidance and power? Is this a group of Christian soldiers being armed and briefed for warfare or just a group of people asking favours? Are they wanting to be used by God or trying to use him?

These are some of the questions this book will try to

answer, and we will meet all those prayer requests again in later chapters.

What prayer isn't

We have seen that prayer is not a device for obtaining benefits and favours from God. Far from being a way of persuading God to do *our* will, it is, or should be, a way of our learning his will – and being given the strength to obey it.

Prayer is not a demonstration of our piety. Jesus made that very plain when he told the story of a Pharisee and a tax collector who both went into the temple in Jerusalem to pray. The Pharisee recited his virtues (no doubt quite truthfully) while the tax collector (who was presumably as much a rogue as all the others who collected taxes for the Roman occupying power) simply admitted his sin and asked for mercy. The Pharisee expected nothing from his prayer but self-satisfaction, and that's all he got. The tax collector asked for life-changing forgiveness and received that. The Pharisee said his prayers; the tax collector prayed.

The preconditions for prayer

It hardly needs to be said that if we want our praying to be effective, the attitude in which we come to God is vital. We must be aware of our *weakness*. In this world, we tend to despise weakness and rate strength very highly. Before God, we must be ready to admit that there is so much that we just can't do. We come to God with empty hands, asking him, not to supplement our slender resources, but to work through us in his mighty power.

We come in our *ignorance.* As Abraham Lincoln put it, 'I have many times been driven to my knees by the utter conviction that I had nowhere else to go.' Our human knowledge, like our human strength, can be woefully inadequate. Left to ourselves, we'd get it wrong time and time again.

We must come *trustfully.* When we lay our burdens on the Lord, we leave them there. That's what he means us to do. We can then get on with doing what we can while God does what we can't. We often hear people say, when they are anxious about something, 'We must pray *extra hard* about this.' As an indication of their concern, it is understandable, but if it implies that God sometimes needs pressure to be put on him, like US army officers in films barking 'and that's an order' to hapless GIs, then it is a mistake. God never needs pushing; he can be trusted.

We must be totally *honest.* God is quite shockproof, and we can – in fact, must – open our hearts completely. There's no need to do a 'vicar's tea party' act where we examine every word we say. When Teresa of Avila prayed, 'From silly devotions and sour-faced saints, good Lord, deliver us', she was being honest. (Perhaps she was also being a bit unkind, but no-one is perfect in this life, even those who get canonized.)

Because prayer is a spiritual exercise, it cannot be governed by, or measured by, human standards. For example, two hours spent in prayer are not necessarily twice as valuable as one. One moment of real contact with God can be more worthwhile than hours of mere pious recitation. That is not to say that we shouldn't be ready to give plenty of time to praying. We should, if only because our rather earthbound natures do not centre on God and his purposes as readily or as quickly as we would like.

As Samuel Chadwick said, 'Hurry is the death of prayer.' If we want to spend with God only the few minutes we can spare after other priorities have been dealt with, we cannot be surprised if we fail to make contact. When we *do* make contact, then we actually become surrounded by our Father's love, aware of Jesus as our friend, and filled with the Spirit's power. In fact, we can say that each time we genuinely open our hearts to our heavenly Father, whatever else we may experience by way of an answer to our prayer, one thing is certain to happen: he will draw us a little closer to himself. That is the same as saying that we increasingly have the 'mind of Christ our Saviour'.

There can be few human activities more worthwhile than that.

Chapter 2

Promises! Promises!

If you go to a prayer meeting or housegroup regularly (and I hope you do, because they are a valuable resource for spiritual growth), you will probably agree that the majority of prayers begin with a sentence or two of praise and thanksgiving followed by one, or perhaps several, or perhaps many, requests. As Christians, we are encouraged to bring our requests, both for ourselves and for others, to God in prayer. But this one-stop spiritual shopping has its dangers as well as its blessings.

There are Christians who claim that God will give you *anything* you ask for in prayer. They will say, 'Yes, and so he will. It says so quite clearly in the Bible. Look at John's gospel, chapter 14 and verse 14: "If you ask me for anything in my name, I will do it." That's plain enough, isn't it? Or turn over to chapter 15 at verse 16: "You did not choose me; I chose you and appointed you to go and bear much fruit … And so the Father will give you whatever you ask of him in my name." Or turn the page again to chapter 16, verse 23: "I am telling you the truth: the Father will give you whatever you ask him for in my name". Back in Matthew's gospel, there is a similar verse in chapter 21, verse 22: "If you believe, you will receive whatever you ask for in prayer. " There you are! The Bible is God's Word, isn't it? And God keeps his promises, doesn't he? How can you say the Bible is not true? Of course God will give you anything you ask – it's just a matter of faith.'

Just?

Is it true that God's giving is proportional to our believing? Not really, because there is no such thing as partly believing. You believe or you don't. If you half believe, it means you are keeping your options open 'just in case'. But the essence of faith is being ready to put the weight of your thought and action on to your faith; you stand or fall by it.

It may be that you are not *100%* convinced; that you still have some residual doubts. As fallen creatures, with two natures still warring within us, we all have sympathy with the man who brought his son to Jesus for healing. He cried, 'I do have faith, but not enough. Help me to have more!' Like him, our feelings are liable to seesaw between confidence and doubt. We should therefore always remember that trusting God is not a feeling, it's a decision. It's the feeling we *act on* that counts.

The writer of the letter to the Hebrews declared that faith was 'to be certain of the things we cannot see' and went on to write about many Old Testament characters who had staked their lives on trusting God. So we must be careful when we talk about praying in faith. Faith – the sort that will take the weight of our actions – is a very rare commodity. It always was, but it is especially so in our present materialistic world. Be careful about saying, 'All you need is faith'; that faith barrier can be enormous.

But not insurmountable. Faith is available to us because it is one of the gifts of the Holy Spirit. Once we understand that faith is God-given, we realize that we are totally dependent on God, whereas an 'anything you ask' attitude suggests that the power to achieve – and decide what to achieve – is in our hands. It isn't; and that's just as well.

Have you ever stopped to think what it would be like if God *did* give us, or do for us, everything we asked? At first sight, it sounds marvellous. If we had a headache, we could get rid of it at once, and in the same way we could be free from all other illnesses, even terminal ones. We could be prosperous, popular, and, if we wished, famous. Our team would win all its matches and our party win every election. All our family and friends would become Christians and prayer letters from missionaries would report conversions by the thousand. The sun would always shine by day and our gardens would be gently watered every night. In our idyllic world, we would promptly deal with any signs of ageing, and teenagers wouldn't even have to put up with acne!

There is no point in pursuing this fantasy. Even if we tried really hard to pray unselfishly, it still wouldn't work. We all have fallen natures, so that, if we were given God's power (because that's what it would mean,

God taking instructions from us), we would easily convince ourselves that what we wanted was for the best. But what would happen if two people made requests that were mutually exclusive? We can all see only too well that if we had God's power without his wisdom, the results would be disastrous.

The fact is that the problems in the world, from minor irritations like dandruff to devastating problems like bereavement or serious accidents, are inevitable and inescapable. We can and should do all we can to eliminate them, but their complete eradication must await the coming of the kingdom of God, the final consummation of God's creation.

Now we must take a closer look at the phrase that occurred in all three of the verses quoted earlier from John's gospel – 'in my name'. This phrase is all too often regarded as merely the small print at the end of the contract when it is in fact the essence of it. It is a built-in acknowledgment that we should not ask for or expect anything that we do not believe Jesus would want us to pray for.

Although we have to admit that our earthbound minds find it difficult to understand just what Jesus would want us to pray for, it is still easy to see how this little phrase can severely curtail our more selfish requests. It does not for a moment limit either God's power or his willingness, but once we appreciate its significance it can transform spiritual begging into a thrilling co-operation with God.

To understand this, take another look at John 16:23. The context of the passage is that Jesus is pointing out to the disciples that he will shortly be leaving them. He is warning them that he will not be around to answer all their questions, but that the Holy Spirit will. So we can read the verse like this: 'When that day comes, you will not ask *me* for anything. I am telling you the truth: the *Father* will give you whatever you ask him for *in my name*.' That is, they were to go on asking as before, but to the Father, through Jesus, once they could no longer ask Jesus himself.

And what sort of things do we suppose they would have been used to asking Jesus for? To understand about God and his purposes; for insights into their own hearts and minds; for the ability to recognize and overcome temptation; to know about judgment, heaven and hell; for healing, both for themselves and others? Yes, all of these. For money, fame, power, protection? We don't know, of course, but what do you think?

I suggest that they asked for spiritual knowledge and resources, and for material *needs*, but their time with Jesus had taught them not to ask for worldly success or comfort. We are living many centuries later, but we are disciples too.

To encourage Christians to use prayer as a means of obtaining anything they want is a bit like the junk mail with which we have become so familiar. Along with colourful leaflets will be a letter congratulating you on having won a car or a large sum of money. It is addressed to you by name and states clearly that all you have to do is claim your prize. Yet somehow or other, when you look further, you find there are some very restricting conditions. So much so that although the letters are sent out by the tens of thousands, not many of those cars actually get delivered.

Most people have now got the measure of these sales techniques and only the very gullible or very greedy are taken in by them. The 'anything you ask' doctrine needs the same scrutiny.

The idea that prayer is a universal provider is so misleading, dangerous and debilitating, especially to young Christians, that it must be refuted. It suggests that we can tell God what to do. We can't. No matter how strong our faith, how unselfish our motives and how sincere our convictions, we must learn that God's will is sovereign, not ours.

One disadvantage of trying to use prayer as an on-tap spiritual resource is that it can weaken our spiritual stamina. There are churches where the emphasis on prayer for healing or other benefits is so marked that life seems to be nothing but problems. Where are the Christians whose spiritual maturity is so strong that they face the difficulties of life – illness, stress at work, redundancy, family difficulties, bereavement – with a calm trust and steady faith? They are found in most churches, but often go almost unnoticed; they are the ones whose *frequent and regular* contact with God enables them to cope with problems as they arise.

It is good to spend some time *every day* in a spiritual work-out of prayer and Bible study, building up our understanding of God. For some people, however, this routine of 'reading the Scripture portion' can easily become a duty, then a chore, and then a burden. They are bored if they do it and guilty if they don't. When that is the case, change the routine but don't abandon the principle; find one that works for you.

None of this should discourage us from praying; quite the reverse. I hope this book will encourage you to pray more, not less. Constant contact with our Father in heaven is vital to the health and effectiveness of our spiritual lives. But we may need to shift the emphasis from what we want to what God is trying to tell us, from things that make us comfortable to things that make us useful.

Nor should challenging the apparent meaning of a text cause us to doubt the truth of the Bible, although it may cause us to dig a bit deeper and search a bit wider to find 'the truth concealed within thy Word' as the hymn says. The Bible is the true and living Word of God. We discover from it that God is a Father who loves and cares for his children, always wants the best for them and always keeps his promises.

To illustrate some of the principles involved in prayer, let us take the situation in Northern Ireland as an example. For many years now, Christians, including me, have prayed for an end to the sectarian killings in the province. It hasn't happened. Why?

We are left with four possible conclusions:

1. Not one of those praying has had enough faith to believe that God is able to achieve the desired result.
2. It isn't God's will that the violence should end.
3. God is unable to bring it about.
4. We do not pray *in Jesus' name.*

Let's look at each of these in turn:

1. No doubt many people have prayed on a 'might as well ask' basis, not really expecting anything to happen. (To be honest, how often do any of us pray

for something and have the real conviction that we will wake up in the morning to find that it has happened?) But surely there have been many others, over the years, who never doubted God's power to transform the situation, and even came to a point where they truly believed that what they asked for would be granted. No, it's not lack of believing prayer.

2. As for whether it is God's will that violence should end, of course it is. It is inconceivable that God could want anything other than harmony and peaceful co-existence. So it's not that.

3. Nor is it because the situation is beyond God's power. His ability to achieve whatever he chooses must be something no Christian would question.

4. That's it! We pray for an end to violence because *we* want peace, without trying to discern God's will. (Yes, of course we know that he wants peace, every bit as much as we do, but not by overriding human will.) We must ask why the violence is there. It is because many thousands of people, in most respects friendly and compassionate, are locked into a sectarian divide that narrows their minds and hardens their hearts. The gunmen or bombers make the headlines, but who supports and encourages them? Who equips them, arms them and shelters them? It is true that most Irish people want peace, but they keep their heads down. As a result, the sectarianism and fear of the majority keep fuelling the hatred and hostility of the minority.

At the time of writing, we cannot tell whether the peace process on which politicians have worked so hard will resolve the conflict. As yet, no swords have been beaten into ploughshares and the invective used by the leaders of the opposing factions shows that their views are as implacable as ever. While they cannot contemplate anything less than victory without compromise, the goal of a lasting peace (when enemies become friends) is not in sight.

Fortunately there are wonderful exceptions who demonstrate a real spirit of Christlike love. Gordon Wilson, whose daughter Marie, a nurse, was killed in the Remembrance Day bombing in Enniskillen, was one of them. There are many in Northern Ireland who honour him; not enough who emulate him.

That this is true can be seen in the case of a Catholic priest and a Presbyterian minister in Limavady, County Derry. Their churches faced each other across the street, and on Christmas morning in 1983 the priest, Father Kevin Mullan, and the minister, the Rev. David Armstrong, exchanged greetings in each other's churches. For this, the minister was censured by his elders. The matter was taken up – and blown up, of course – by the media, and eventually he found himself unable to continue his ministry. He had to resign, and he moved to England. He had not deviated in any way from his Protestant faith and principles; he had simply wanted to express Christian love at the season of goodwill. Some of his flock and many of his colleagues saw him as a traitor. Effectively, they drove him out.

Applying this to our prayers for Northern Ireland, we have to ask ourselves exactly what we are praying for. What, if anything, do we expect to see happen? Are we asking for a radical, and sudden, change of heart and mind (or, if you like, of attitude and belief) by a large proportion of the citizens of Northern Ireland? If we are, do we expect to see it happen?

I do not question for one moment that God could achieve just that, but do we really think he will? Is it in line with our experience, with what we know of the way God's Holy Spirit works? It is like praying that all their faults will disappear overnight, so that they awake in the morning with unselfish love for all their fellow citizens – 'neighbours' was the word Jesus used.

None of this should lead us to the conclusion that we are wasting our time in praying for peace in Northern Ireland. As with many of our prayers, we have to remind ourselves that God's power is not limited to our expectations.

God could bring about a radical and sudden change, easily, but it runs counter to all we know of Him. He could have made all people without the ability to sin in the first place – but he didn't. It is clearly part of his plan that we should all strive to know and follow his will while still retaining our freedom of choice – our ability to reject, or even rebel against, the very God who created us.

So the problem of violence in Northern Ireland is not a question of a few terrorists who need to be reformed or eradicated, but a situation in which many thousands of people stand in need of being made loving by the influence and power of the Holy Spirit.

And that's the situation everywhere on earth. There are plenty of places where long-running animosity finds a convenient excuse (colour, race, religion, politics, class or tradition) to erupt into violence. The Middle East, the former Soviet Union, and parts of Africa come to mind, but other places may be in the headlines when you read this.

The very intractability of such situations surely means we should pray more often and more fervently, not less. We should also pray more intelligently and realistically. That may well mean that we spend far more time and thought on deciding what to ask God for than we spend asking. And we must, as with all our prayers, be ready to be challenged into action if we find any way at all in which we can be involved in practical ways.

We cannot use prayer as an easy way to solve or avoid problems, whether personal or global. A certain Joshua Ward once prayed, 'O Lord, thou knowest I have nine houses in the City of London, and have lately purchased an estate in Essex. I beseech thee to preserve these counties from earthquakes and fire.' Few of us are likely to pray as selfishly as that, but sometimes we need reminding that, in the words of Henry Emerson Fosdick, 'God is not a cosmic bell-boy for whom we can press a button to get things done.'

Prayer is more than asking God to run errands for us. Rather it is a process of tuning our minds to that of our heavenly Father, so that we can be used for his purposes. The vast spiritual resources of God's love and power are available, and God longs to use them, working through us. We should be equally willing for that to happen. But that involves more – much more – than a constant stream of requests.

Before we begin to look at the way God responds to our praying, we must look in greater detail at the activity involved in praying, both on our own and with others.

Chapter 3

How to pray alone

'I want to pray. I know I should pray. So how do I start? Do I kneel or sit or stand? Do I address God as Lord, or Father, or what?'

Wait a minute! You're asking the wrong questions. You're assuming there are rules to be obeyed and procedures to be followed. There aren't. Prayer should be natural. So that it can be, here are a few basic facts to remember:

1. We are going to spend time with our Father. Sadly, there are many people today whose relationship with their human father has been so painful, or even non-existent, that this thought may not appeal. But we can be sure that *this* Father loves us deeply.

2. He's waiting for us to call. He's got a welcoming smile on his face. There's no password and no dragon of a secretary outside his office door, as with human VIPs.

3. He doesn't mind what we call him so long as we say it in humble love.

4. He doesn't care what posture we adopt so long as we find it helpful and not distracting.

So now you can go ahead.

'But what do I say?'

We've already seen that we don't necessarily have to say anything at all so long as our thoughts are on God and open to God. In practice, it may help to put our thoughts into words because that is how we are used to expressing ourselves, so words may prove helpful, but God can read us anyway. The vital thing is to begin any time of prayer by centring our thoughts on God and not on ourselves. We contemplate his almighty power and love; we just rejoice that we are in his presence.

We may have difficulty in feeling that we are in the presence of God. The answer to that problem, as with many other difficulties of Christian living, is to remember that facts matter more than feelings; God *is* with us whether we feel it or not.

If you ever find yourself doubting whether you are acceptable to God, read again what is called the story of the prodigal son (although perhaps it ought to be called the story of the perfect father). Just imagine that boy's thoughts as he approached his father with trepidation, only to be welcomed with open arms.

Once we are sure of God's presence and confident of his loving attention, we are beginning to pray. How we go on will depend on our personalities, our situation (whether we are experiencing great blessing in our lives or have great needs), and how the Holy Spirit guides us. Because we are all different, our ways of praying will be different too. We each need to find patterns of prayer that suit our personalities and meet our needs.

But if we can't make rules, and shouldn't try to, it may still be helpful to suggest an outline we can follow. I would advocate that we should normally move from praise to confession to thanksgiving to intercession, ending with more praise. This is surely how a meeting with very dear human friends would progress. We would greet them warmly; then if we thought we had done anything to hurt them, we would say we were sorry before we went any further. We would thank them for things they had given us or done for us. Then, and only then, we would ask for help, whether for others or ourselves. And we would express the warmth of our feelings again as we said goodbye.

Another very natural way of beginning a time of prayer, if it is evening, is to go over the events of that day. Think of things done (or perhaps not done!), people met, and so on. That is almost sure to raise topics for both thanksgiving and confession. Prayer early in the day provides the opportunity to consider the events and duties ahead, possibly asking for guidance, wisdom or whatever.

I suspect (probably because it's true in my case) that the biggest hindrance to prayer is distraction. The more we try to concentrate on our heavenly Father, the more we become aware of our earthly surroundings. If you remember A. A. Milne's song 'Christopher Robin is Saying his Prayers', you will recall how easily young Christopher was distracted by seeing Nanny's dressing gown through his fingers or recalling the 'fun in the bath tonight'. That syndrome is by no means confined to little boys. A welter of thoughts and ideas try to claim our attention; all too often they succeed.

Gerard Hughes, in his book *Oh God, Why?*, suggests that instead of desperately trying to banish these distractions, we should accept them and incorporate them into our prayers. This is helpful, because the more we try to fight off unwanted thoughts, the more insistent they become. Some discipline will still be needed, though, if daydreaming is to be avoided. One simple idea is to jot down a few notes on a scrap of paper; and other suggestions are given below. First, though, let me mention some common ways of focusing attention which should be treated with a good deal of caution.

Some people try to use meditation techniques derived from eastern religions, such as breath control or the repetition of mantras. The idea is that the discipline involved helps them to concentrate their minds, but there is a danger. As practised in Hinduism, a mantra is a prescribed formula taken from the *Vedas*, their scriptures in the Sanskrit language. It may be a single syllable or a longer passage, and is given by a guru, along with instruction on its recitation. Hindus claim that reciting a mantra in this way releases magical powers, a view that no Christian could accept.

This is equally true even if the name of Jesus is used as a mantra, something that is occasionally heard in a prayer meeting. Much as we invoke the Holy Spirit when we pray, our minds must be actively involved throughout. Any suggestion of raising spiritual awareness by the use of hypnosis, drugs or any similar means must be firmly repudiated.

Others prefer to use a rosary, an icon, or a statuette. This is more satisfactory, but can still pose some danger in that the item used can itself become an object of veneration, in which case it does more harm than good. But on the whole, something to look at or handle can be a useful aid to concentration.

The obvious and best choice is the Bible. There can be few things more spiritually nourishing than having our eyes fixed on Scripture while our hearts are centred on God. We can think of it as God speaking to us through his Word at the same time as he is guiding us by his Spirit.

There are plenty of other possibilities. We rarely think of reading hymns, but many of them are full of deep truth, beautifully expressed. For this purpose, the tune doesn't matter; the quality of the poetry does. For example, try reading Samuel Crossman's hymn, 'My song is love unknown' very slowly and thoughtfully. As you do, imagine that you are watching Jesus at his trial and crucifixion.

A prayerbook can be used in the same way, as can some of the many books of prayers that you will find in your local Christian bookshop. Books of prayers vary greatly, each designed for a different readership, so take time to browse until you find those that suit you. You could also use one of the 'Through the Year' books with a devotional reading for each day, or a book of Christian poetry.

Isaac Newton once wrote, 'I can get my telescope and look millions of miles into space; but I can go into my room and in prayer get nearer to God and heaven than I can when assisted by all the telescopes of earth.' Perhaps he found God more readily in his room because he had just been looking at his creation through a telescope. Certainly, whenever I have had the opportunity to look through a microscope or high-powered magnifier at, say, a petal or an insect's wing, I have found myself marvelling afresh at the wonder of God's creation.

Pictures can help, too. Not just biblical or religious ones. Photos of family, close friends or missionaries can be valuable aids to guiding our thoughts, as can prayer letters from people on active Christian service.

Music can also help us to pray. Some people play a praise tape, while others prefer to listen to, say, the Albinoni *Adagio* or Widor's *Toccata* – or you might prefer Enya. There is a danger here, though, and that is that we can simply enjoy the music for its own sake instead of using it as a means of lifting our thoughts to God.

Another possibility for prompting our prayers is to have a newspaper in front of us. That should provide us with almost unlimited topics for intercession. So many, in fact, that we could easily become depressed. We may need to remind ourselves of the words of the Victorian poet and novelist Jean Ingelow: 'I am glad to think I am not bound to make the world go right, but only to discover and to do, with cheerful heart, the work that God appoints.'

Above all, forget yourself and what you want to say; concentrate on God and what he wants to hear. I say 'on God', but some people prefer to address their prayers to Jesus. There is not the slightest reason why you shouldn't if you find it more natural. This is not the place to give a dissertation on the Trinity, so I'll just say that your prayers will get through!

Whatever you do, spend time over it; contemplation cannot be hurried. If you have a book that you are using, read a few lines, ponder them, and let them lead you into thinking about God – his power, his love and his wisdom. (Try it with Psalm 8, for example, or Philippians 2:1–11.) It doesn't matter whether you are kneeling, sitting or standing, or whether your eyes are open or closed. It does matter that you are somewhere quiet and without distractions.

If contemplation of God doesn't lead you naturally into confession and repentance, you must be unusual. A true awareness of God's holiness is sure to make us conscious of our unworthiness and our failures. There are two problems with confession. The first is that it can easily become a meaningless formula; we can all too easily describe ourselves as miserable sinners, or even, as the Psalmist once did, as a worm, without ever feeling contrite. Confession must be specific enough to hurt if it is to be effective; we must call to mind particular acts, words or thoughts of which we are ashamed.

The other problem with confession can be an unhealthy guilt complex. Confession is for our sins to be dealt with, not mulled over.

Lifted by worship, humbled by penitence and cleansed by forgiveness, we are ready for thanksgiving. This part of our praying should be easy. There are always so many good things, material and spiritual, for which we can and should thank God. That will be true even in times of illness, sorrow or depression. From time to time, it is good to make a point of thanking God for those things we often take for granted, such as loved ones, or sight, or music, or a good appetite.

We also do well occasionally to promise God that we will still praise him even if any great blessing is taken from us. The last three verses of the book of Habakkuk will show you what I mean.

Having said 'Sorry' and 'Thank you', we can now say 'Please'; and our prayer requests will be divided into our own needs and intercession for others. (In ordinary speech, intercession usually means 'putting in a good word for someone', but in the church it refers to prayers offered for people who are ill or in any other kind of need.) Here too, we must avoid making rules, but it is safe to say that if our requests far outweigh our praise and gratitude, and, especially if our prayers for ourselves exceed those for others, we should check whether we are not putting our wants before God's will. It is a very easy thing to do.

'Asking prayers' are considered in detail later, but we should note here that the attitude in which we make our requests is important. If we ask God for anything, we must believe that he *can* do as we ask. That does not mean that we presume he *will.* We can, however, be sure that he will do what is right. That in turn means that once we have laid a burden before God, we can leave it there. We should not keep on carrying it.

Before concluding our time of prayer, it is good to offer more praise, if only to remind ourselves of God's power to do all we ask, and his love and wisdom to know what is in our best interests.

I have said that prayer should be natural, but that is not to say that it can be taken lightly. John Blanchard points out that 'we are encouraged to come freely to God but not flippantly'. It's *simple* enough – it's talking with God – but it's not *easy*. In fact, there are times when it can be a very demanding spiritual exercise. We may need to agonize before God if we are praying for a situation that deeply disturbs us. It has been said that prayer that costs nothing is worth nothing, and Martin Luther described it as 'the sweat of the soul'. When Abraham was pleading for God to have mercy on Sodom, he had to work really hard, but it did pay off.

Fortunately for us, God is very patient. Jonah got cross with God and Elijah once had the sulks, but because that was how they honestly felt, God allowed them to get it off their chests without condemning them.

We must always remember that prayer is talking *with* God, not just *to* him. The listening is by far the hardest part. Fulton Sheen put it well when he said, 'Most commit the same mistake with God that they do with their friends; they do all the talking.' This is because we find it so hard to get out of the way of thinking that talking must consist of two people saying words to each other. So we fill in all the silences. If only we could keep in mind our definition of prayer as letting God read our thoughts and reshape them to his will, then we might leave more space in which God can 'speak'.

When should we pray? We know we can pray at any time but that very fact can be a danger. Because we don't have to keep appointments with God at fixed times, it is easy not to keep them at all, or, at least, not until we need to. We know what happens when we invite acquaintances to pop in for coffee *at any time*; they never come. If we'd made a date, they would have kept it.

We have all heard the maxim, 'Seven days without prayer make one weak'. So there are sound practical reasons for setting aside regular times for prayer, however much they may be supplemented by additional times of thanksgiving or supplication.

For many Christians, the time for prayer is bedtime. This is good in that it focuses our minds on God just before we go to sleep. It is less good if we are too tired to think about what we are doing. In that case, first thing in the morning may be a better time. C. S. Lewis wrote: 'The moment you wake up each morning, all your wishes and hopes for the day rush at you like wild animals. And the first job each morning consists in shoving it all back; in listening to that other voice, taking that other point of view, letting that other, larger, stronger, quieter life come flowing in.'

So then, we can pray morning or evening, or, better still, both, or at any other time. It depends partly on when we are most alert (or least dozy!) and partly on when there will be the fewest distractions. Mothers at home, with children at school or nursery, often like a quiet time as soon as husband and children are out of the way.

Where should we pray? My daughter says she can pray best when taking a long walk in the park, and I know of others who like to pray in the garden or when walking the dog. The only necessary criterion is that it should be somewhere quiet where we will not be disturbed.

It is worth taking some trouble to find the times and places for prayer that best suit your personality and your circumstances. But whenever, wherever and however we pray, three requirements will be paramount.

One is a sense of *awe*. We have the joy and honour of being God's children, but we must never let familiarity diminish our reverence.

The second is a sense of *need*. We know that we can't give God anything; whatever we have, he gave us, and whatever we are, he made us. So before him, we will always stand in need. We come with open hands, ready to receive all that he has to give. Yet in a sense, there are two things we *can* give to God, and what's more, our giving them will delight him. One is our love. He is our Father, after all, and what father is not thrilled when his children show their love for him? The other is time. This is something we have to dispose of as we choose; we can spend it on ourselves or devote it to others, including our heavenly Father.

The last is complete *openness*. Even the best of us are so used to telling other people only as much as we want them to know, that we may forget the obvious fact that God knows us better than we know ourselves. We cannot conceal anything from him, but it is still important that we shouldn't want to. We may not even realize it, but we can come to prayer concealing things even from ourselves. Our prayer needs to include asking for self-awareness and honesty.

The vital point to remember is that we are not despatching messages to God, but spending time in his presence. If we can keep that in mind, we will be more ready to keep that appointment and more reluctant to end it. Indeed, the best point at which to end a time of prayer is when there is a practical duty that rightly claims our attention, whether it is changing the baby's nappy, mowing the lawn, cooking the dinner, or getting some sleep. Meanwhile, our thoughts will be less likely to wander, and we will be more ready to open our minds for God to fill them with his truth, love and power.

Chapter 4

How to pray with others

Much as we need private prayer times, we also need to find – or make – opportunities to pray with fellow Christians. Prayer meetings, whether small or large, have that extra quality of fellowship that our own quiet times lack. And just in case you think fellowship is just a churchy word for friendship, it isn't. Fellowship is the bond that binds believers to Christ and to each other, and that unity of heart and mind lifts our hearts and strengthens our faith.

Some prayers may be too personal to include in such times, but others will be all the more effective for being shared. For one thing, the group can seek God's will *together* as to what they should be praying about. If one member wants to ask God for something thoughtlessly or selfishly, the others will (or should, if they have learnt to be honest with each other, in love) gently question whether it is an unwise or improper request.

It may be that two or more members of the group will have the same concern on their minds. This will help the group to focus on that issue and pray with more earnestness and purpose, and will possibly result in those who raised the matter meeting together for more prayer another time.

There is a practical discipline involved in praying with others in that we have to make sure that all can hear and understand what is being said. This is particularly true of a time of prayer in a hall or large room, but even in a small group it can still be a problem. The quiet ones may need to be gently reminded that if others cannot hear their prayer, they will not be able to share in it as they want to.

However careful you are to avoid it, it may still happen at times that someone fails to hear as another is praying. In fact, only last evening that happened at the housegroup I was at. One woman was praying when another woman in the opposite corner of the room, and obviously a bit hard of hearing, also started to pray. Sensitively, the first woman stopped speaking, and, when the second had finished, carried on with her own prayer as if nothing had happened. Nobody was put out by it in the least.

Another problem is that some find it very hard to pray aloud in front of others. It should be made clear to the group that everyone is encouraged to join in the prayers and that it doesn't matter one bit if their prayers are short or not beautifully phrased. No-one will mind, including God. At the same time, it is important that people should never be allowed to feel inferior if they don't or can't respond. You may not hear them, but God can.

As with private prayer, it is good to let our times of corporate prayer follow naturally from a time of worship or Bible study, however brief. This helps us to fix our thoughts on God and his power rather than on ourselves and our desires.

One advantage of praying with others is that sharing our concerns in this way should prompt us to give practical help where we can. For example, if you have prayed for someone who is old and lonely – and many are – you may then decide to pay that person a visit. That may be a case of two prayers being answered; yours, because you stated a need and God guided you to do something about it; and the prayer of the person you visited.

Prayer meetings or housegroups are sometimes unsure how to deal with prayer requests that remain largely unchanged from week to week, possibly for months. There seems to be nothing new to say. So don't try to say it; there are no prizes for finding twenty different ways of saying the same thing. Here, however, is one suggestion for keeping those regular prayer requests in mind. The leader can say that there will be a time of meditation, during which various names or situations can be mentioned. No details need be given because they are all known, and the members can each offer their own prayers in silence.

The biggest single barrier to meeting for prayer is finding the time to do it. Ask any minister if he or she finds it easy to get people to prayer meetings; everyone will agree that it's a good idea, but only a few will come. Admittedly, time is often the excuse rather than the reason, but it is still difficult to fit prayer meetings into busy lives.

This sometimes results in prayer meetings being arranged at very unusual times. Prayer breakfasts are often popular with young people, but less so with parents who have to get children off to school and themselves off to work.

Another suggestion that is often made is a night of prayer, or a prayer vigil, especially in time of crisis or great need. What needs to be clearly understood is that God doesn't give Brownie points for praying at odd hours or for long periods, so if you think that God is impressed by our praying in the small hours, forget it. But the discipline of giving prayer a place of importance above comfort and convenience is another matter altogether. That can be really valuable.

Staying in Amman some years ago, I was awakened at 4am by the cry of the muezzin from a nearby minaret calling the faithful to prayer. (It was a recorded call, of course; it was all right for him!) I had been told that a translation of part of his message was 'Prayer is better than sleep.' I must say that I was disinclined to believe it at that hour, but in a Christian context we know that Jesus would have endorsed the statement wholeheartedly because he would often spend all night in prayer, and still be ready for work the next morning. And if Jesus felt the need to pray like that, surely we do.

There are two problems we frequently encounter in prayer meetings. One is a tendency to make prayers so vague that we aren't really sure of their purpose. I can remember in my distant youth hearing very long prayers that consisted of a succession of biblical or other Christian phrases strung together. They were all-purpose prayers, with no relevance to the work of the church or anyone in it, let alone the world outside it. They were sincere and genuine enough, but unrelated to real life.

The other problem is the opposite: to tell God in great detail not only what to do but how to do it. Many times, when people have been praying for healing, I have heard them explain with full clinical details what treatment was being administered and why, and what stage had been reached, and point out to God exactly what he had to do next. God could have been left in no doubt about his duty. What was in doubt was whose will was paramount.

Sometimes, a prayer can need explanation for the benefit of others present who are unaware of the background detail. It is usually best to preface a time of prayer with topics being suggested by the group, who will give any necessary details. If someone subsequently decides to pray on another topic, however, it may well be possible to give any necessary explanation in the prayer. For example, 'I pray for my colleague, Jennifer, whose mother is beginning a course of chemotherapy.' That will be perfectly clear, even if further information is given afterwards. In other cases, there is no reason at all why someone should not give a sentence or two of explanation before addressing God in prayer. It need not have any adverse effect on the spirit of reverence in the group.

In our typical prayer meeting in chapter 1, Derek's

prayer for a job is an example of where we can fall into the trap of giving God orders. Derek was absolutely right, and so were those with him, in sharing his need for work with his Father in heaven. What would not have been right is specifying the type of work, salary and fringe benefits! For all he knew, God had an entirely new career planned for him.

The problem of vague prayers is more common, and an example of it was Rachel's asking for prayer for Africa. Was she thinking of famine victims, racial harmony, or something else? It was necessary to be more explicit, not because God didn't know or couldn't deal with more than one problem per prayer, but because all those present (not just Rachel) needed to think about what they were praying for. That is because prayer is not a way of unloading problems on to God, but of getting our minds and wills into line with his, and we can't do that if we are not sure what problems we are dealing with. We cannot discharge our obligations as easily as that. God wants us to think about the world and its needs and our part, however small, in meeting them.

Perhaps the best advice that can be given in this connection is to be wary of using the word 'bless'. There's nothing wrong with the word, of course, but it does get used rather carelessly. What does 'Lord, bless our vicar' mean? Cheer him up? (After all, the word means 'to make happy'.) Improve his sermons? Encourage him? It probably means, 'Continue to fill him with the enabling power of the Holy Spirit', in which case it may be better to say just that.

In the same way, 'Bless Helen in Brazil' suggests that

not enough is known about her situation. One of the tasks of a prayer meeting is to share news so that prayer can have more meaning. If someone knows that Helen is facing language or cultural or political problems, or is worried about her family at home, then prayer for her will have more point. This is a case in which news should be shared before beginning to pray if possible. But beware! It is all too easy for a time of sharing to eat heavily into the time that should be spent praying.

In this connection, anyone leading a prayer meeting must be careful to avoid gossip and be sensitive when dealing with delicate personal issues. It is sometimes necessary to say, 'I think that is something we should not be discussing here.'

One tip that leaders of prayer meetings may find useful at times is to suggest that for the first part of the available prayer time, nobody *asks* for anything. To use the 'teaspoon' system (tsp) much used in Sunday schools and family services, they can say 'thank you' and 'sorry' but not 'please'. Or, to revert to another acronym which is sometimes used – ACTS (the letters stand for adoration, confession, thanksgiving and supplication) – it can be suggested that the supplication (a churchy word for asking) should be saved for another time.

Laying on of hands

Many Christians are puzzled by the significance of laying hands on someone for whom prayer is being offered. Perhaps more ought to be puzzled by it, because I have met very few who can explain why we do it. It seems that some do it simply because it was done in the early church. For others, it seems to be an additive to make the prayer more powerful.

As with all things spiritual, mere gestures, like mere repetition of words, have no power. The significance is in what is being expressed by the action. The act of laying on of hands is a sign that you are earnestly seeking and appropriating God's power for a particular purpose. It is therefore used on such occasions as confirmation, ordination and valediction – as when the church at Antioch sent out Barnabas and Saul on their first missionary journey.

It is also done with prayers for healing or spiritual gifts. Here again, it provides no magic powers, but it can be a valuable visual aid, stressing the importance of the prayer being offered.

Prayer partners

A prayer partner is someone who pledges to pray regularly for another person or venture. It is not a task to be undertaken lightly, because it demands faithfulness and involves more than just praying. It is not possible to pray consistently and intelligently for, say, a missionary without keeping up to date with how the work is going. That in turn is likely to create an awareness of practical needs which the prayer partner will want to see met.

It *is* a task that can be undertaken by someone who is prevented, perhaps by age or infirmity, from doing other tasks in the church. In fact, the elderly or housebound members of a church are very often a seriously under-used resource. For example, in my own church there was a woman who could never attend church but who would cheerfully fold outreach leaflets, even when there were 3,000 of them. In the same way, others who are not physically active could take on a commitment to uphold the work of the church in prayer. The prayers could be for all manner of people and situations, so long as the prayer partner is given adequate information to pray effectively. That would entail regular visits by a minister or elder to maintain a strong link between the partner and the church.

Prayer chains

A prayer chain is a way of enabling people to meet urgent requests for prayer. The participants each promise to pass prayer requests on by telephone to the next person on the chain as soon as they receive them, as well as praying themselves. They also promise not to vary the message and not to gossip about it. The disadvantage of a prayer chain is that people are not always available, so it will frequently happen that *A* rings *B* who has just gone out shopping. That will involve ringing *C* instead, to avoid delay, and contacting *B* later. A bigger snag is that someone has to decide when a matter is of sufficient importance to justify initiating a round of calls. Unless some judgment is applied, it is possible for the whole system to be debased by a few people constantly making trivial requests.

A variation on the prayer chain is to telephone two or three people and ask each of them to ring two or three more. This is particularly suitable when the first calls are initiated by a group of elders or housegroup leaders who can use discretion as to whom they ring on their 'list'. Such a prayer network is more spontaneous, involves no formal list of participants, and is usually faster in operation.

Prayer triplets

Prayer triplets consist of two people getting together at mutually convenient times to pray for a third person. I have known of such triplets being used to pray for the conversion of a close friend or relative, with the promise that they would not give up until their objective had been achieved. The praying was right because it was positive and clearly focused; the promise was wrong because it was an attempt to set God's agenda.

Similar small prayer groups are sometimes formed in connection with an evangelistic campaign, to support those taking part or to pray for people to respond to the message. They are a valuable reminder that conversions are primarily the work of the Holy Spirit. A campaign can be well organized and well supported, and the preaching clear and forceful, but nothing will happen unless the Spirit moves. It is therefore a sound policy to give time and effort to plead that he will.

Of course, prayer triplets need not be confined to big evangelistic events, and can be used in the ongoing work of junior church, youth movements, Christian Unions in schools or colleges, and many other situations.

All these methods of organizing prayer carry the danger that the emphasis is on asking. It is right to make requests, especially on behalf of others, but even in emergencies we should still find time in our prayers to reflect on God's sovereignty and make sure that we are seeking his will rather than our own wishes.

The listening mode

When we join with other Christians to ask God to guide us, how do we know when, or whether, he has? Sometimes we have even forgotten by the next morning what we asked for, let alone what happened about it. God *never* ignores our prayers, as we shall see later, but we often need to make a conscious effort to be aware of his response. We should therefore see that there are times of silence in our prayer meetings during which God's Spirit can speak to our hearts. He may speak to one member who will share with the group what he or she has received. That doesn't mean that anyone necessarily hears a voice or sees a vision – although, make no mistake, that can happen. What is more usual is that one or more of the group will be led to say, 'It seems to me that …' That is God answering.

That may lead to further discussion; God will be in that too. In that way, we use our intellects but under God's control. It may be that there is no immediate answer, in which case the matter may be raised again the next time that group meets, until which point it is important that each of them should give that matter a place in their own quiet times. If we talk to our Father, he is sure to answer; we must be sure to give time to receiving it.

Similarly, with prayers for healing and other needs we must keep that concern in our minds, both individually and as a group, until we are aware of how God has responded.

We may find plenty of difficulties in getting together with other Christians to pray. In fact, Satan will make sure we do; that's his job, and he's good at it. It is worth taking the trouble to overcome every obstacle, because our Christian lives will be all the stronger for it.

Praying with children

One aspect of prayer that is sadly neglected in many households is praying with children at home. Some parents teach their children to pray at bedtime while they are very young, but drop the practice before long. One reason for this is that teaching children to pray is far from easy. If you take the fairy-godmother approach, they very soon realize that it doesn't work. If you encourage them to ask but warn them that they may ask in vain, they don't take long to decide that praying is pointless.

What is needed is to get right away from the idea of asking for favours. Give them an awareness that God is real, even if they can't see him; that he knows them and loves them; that he is pleased when they are good and sad when they are bad; and he will help them to be good if they really want to. They won't have to outgrow or unlearn any of that as they get older.

If they prefer to pray to Jesus because they hear stories about him, that's fine. You will probably discover that even very young children can, in their simplicity, understand and accept spiritual concepts almost as well as you can, if not better!

Chapter 5
Praying in church

If you think that when you are in a church service it is the minister's (or vicar's or worship leader's) job to do the praying while you just listen, you've been missing something. Quite a lot, in fact. When he or she says, 'Let *us* pray', the leader means just that. When Christians gather for worship, they join together in prayer. If, as is usual, someone is leading that prayer, he or she is guiding the thinking of the whole congregation. The basic rule that prayer is opening up our minds and hearts to God applies just as much in church as when we are on our own at home. That means that we have to listen carefully to what is being said, or, if it is a liturgical service, think carefully about what we are saying. Only if we do that can the whole church be said to be praying together.

On the question of liturgy (printed material repeated by the congregation), we must make sure that we do not repeat words, however beautiful they are, without thinking about their meaning. It is easy to allow ancient and hallowed words to trigger off a feeling of religious euphoria. This can be dangerous in making us feel righteous when it is better that we should be made aware of our spiritual needs and challenged to do something about them.

When you go to visit close friends, do you always say the same things to them, and in the same words? No, that would be far too sterile. You would talk naturally, saying how you truly felt, and your friends would do the same. It is true that when we are in God's presence we should be more reverent than with a human friend, but we can, and should, talk naturally.

Some churches are beginning to deal with this problem by preparing fresh liturgical material for each service, displaying it on an overhead projector so that the congregation can read the responses. An excellent idea. The fact that the members of the congregation are reading aloud helps them to concentrate, and the fact that they are doing so together emphasizes their unity as a family of believers.

Another growing trend is for times of open prayer in public worship – and not only in charismatic groups. This can be very helpful in allowing people to express their thoughts in such a way that fellow Christians can join with them. It does, however, raise some problems. One is that some of the pray-ers may have very soft voices and be quite inaudible to many of the congregation – if the building is large, to nearly all of them. If a 'roving mike' is available, it may help, except that the sort of person who needs it probably won't use it.

If open prayer in Sunday services is still unusual, inviting people to submit requests for prayer is more common. Sometimes these requests are made during the service, but more often they are collected in some way or other before the service. Such prayers call for sensitive handling by those leading worship, who may be asked to pray for someone they don't know who is in a situation they don't fully understand.

Children should be encouraged to make prayer requests, although this can result in being asked to pray for Nana's corns or a sick goldfish. There is nothing wrong with such prayers and such requests should never be 'put down', because of how much they matter to the one asking, but if there are many of them, it is better that they are dealt with in a small group. That could be in Sunday school, or the children concerned could be prayed with in a corner of the church, then or after the service.

One result of asking for prayer topics is that people are likely to ask for more practical blessings than spiritual ones. (Not that this feature is confined to prayers in church; it applies just as much to praying at home.) A certain Jeremy Taylor, a seventeenth-century parson, gave some good advice on this question. He said: 'For spiritual blessings, be importunate, perpetual, persevering; for temporal, be short, conditional, modest.' 'Importunate' is not a word we use these days, but it means being insistent to the point of being prepared to be a nuisance. In other words, if we are asking God for something that will strengthen our faith, make our witness more effective, and help us grow in grace, we should be prepared to spend time and effort in our quest. And go on doing so. If, however, we are asking for something for our own satisfaction (which doesn't necessarily mean being selfish), we should give it a low priority.

A good way of dealing with requests for prayer of a personal nature, or on matters where confidentially should be respected, is to pray with the person concerned after the service. This is not always easy to arrange. The church may be small and crowded, with children running around, while the people who most need this prayer ministry may be the ones least likely to ask for it.

Don't give up. If a room or side chapel can be set aside for this purpose, so much the better, and it is helpful if someone goes to that place as soon as the service ends, to be available if needed. But if all you can do is designate a corner of the church, settle for that. To persuade people to use this personal prayer ministry, begin the service by saying something like, 'If you have come to church with a deep personal problem, please don't try to handle it alone. There is always someone here who will be glad to pray with you after the service, and confidences will be respected', followed by information on how to get that help. The announcement will need to be repeated until the routine has become familiar, and then from time to time for the benefit of new arrivals.

Be warned, though, that such prayer requests may well be, or include, a cry for help on a human level. So someone should be ready to provide that help as far as possible. The apostle James had something to say about this in his letter (see James 2:14–17).

Now what about requests for prayer that are anything but personal; for people you don't know, in situations far away? These might be the victims of air crashes, sunken ferries, earthquakes, famines or so-called ethnic cleansing. What can you say?

It is obviously right and good that we should express our concern for victims of every kind of suffering and disaster, even if we do not know just who they are and are never likely to. We know that God cares about them, but how can we show that *we* do? By asking for them the same things we would ask if we knew them well: freedom from suffering, fear and shock, and healing – whatever seems to be appropriate in the circumstances. Above all, never let the scale of the disaster evoke the feeling that it's not worth praying.

We cannot consider praying in church without taking account of the fact that many of the hymns we sing are addressed to God (or Jesus or the Holy Spirit), and are therefore prayers. If we are honest, we usually sing hymns for the enjoyment of their tunes rather than for their words. That is a pity, because they are not just musical interludes, and anything that helps to bring out their meaning is to be welcomed.

Some effective ways of doing this are to sing a hymn, or perhaps just a verse, unaccompanied; to meditate on these words while the tune is being played quietly; or to read it instead of singing it. Whatever your brand of churchmanship, the thing to keep in mind is that prayer, wherever or however it is said or sung, is not a mechanical exercise but a means of making active contact with a living God.

Some people find it easier to pray in church than at home. Perhaps it's the surroundings and the silence (unless it's a family service!) that are more conducive to prayer. For others, however, the problem of wandering thoughts and lack of concentration are just as acute in a pew as anywhere else. The only answer is a determination to discipline yourself, bearing in mind the importance – and the privilege – of the activity in which you are engaged.

Remember that however many people may be in that congregation, you are not praying unless *you* have made contact with the living God. When a whole company of people really do *unite* in prayer, however, the atmosphere of worship changes – you can feel it.

It is usual to end prayers with a phrase such as 'through Jesus Christ our Lord' or 'in Jesus' name'. There are good reasons for this. It reminds us that Jesus opened the way for us to address God as our Father, without the need for any priest or other intermediary and without having to go to any special building. It is not important whether we use these or similar words, but it is important that we never lose sight of the meaning behind them.

Not all of our praying in church is corporate prayer. There is that time before the service begins when it is customary (in some traditions at least) to spend a few moments in private prayer. It is easy to allow this to become a habit with little or no meaning, sometimes hardly more than a gesture. If it does, that is a great pity, because those moments can be really important, not only to you but to others.

For example, do you ever pray that God will help

those leading the worship? Your prayers can make a difference to the minister, the organist or musicians, and the Sunday-school teachers. You can also ask for a humble and receptive heart – and to be free from a tendency to criticize!

We all know that the 'day of rest' can include hectic times, especially in families with young children, and getting to church on time can be one of them. So spend the short time before the service to ask for a tranquil mind. These few moments can be precious; use them.

Similarly, the brief time of quiet after the service ends and before the hubbub starts, can be used to absorb what has just taken place and thank God for it. You can reflect on things that were said or sung, and lay the ensuing week before God. Worship is, among other things, a time for refuelling and rearming for the business of living as Christians in a secular world; we do well to make sure we do not go into that world unprepared.

Chapter 6

The first answer: Yes

We know that God doesn't always do as we ask, but it's amazing how often he does. Again and again we will plead with God for something – and receive it. Sometimes we didn't even expect to receive it, so it wasn't our faith that moved God to action but simply his love. We are like a boy who asks for a mountain bike for Christmas, knowing quite well that it is really too much to ask for; but he still receives it, because his parents want to please him.

We are also like the believers in Jerusalem who were having a prayer meeting because their leader, Peter, had been imprisoned. I'm sure they all prayed most fervently and had no doubt at all about God's power to work a miracle to secure his release. Then there was a knock on the door and young Rhoda slipped out to see who it was. It was Peter! Excitedly, she ran back to give the news but was told, in effect, 'Don't be daft, Rhoda, it can't be! Peter is in prison, isn't he?' Even when she insisted, they still disbelieved her. But there was Peter, free! God had said yes.

God loves to say yes. He loves to give us what we want, to help us achieve more than our own resources would allow, to comfort us in times of sorrow, to replenish our faith in times of doubt. Of course he does – he loves us. He is our Father. Right at the beginning of his ministry, in the Sermon on the Mount, Jesus taught that God was more ready than human fathers to give good things to his children.

When Isaac was looking for a wife, Abraham was anxious that he should not marry a Canaanite girl, so he sent his oldest servant, Nahor, to choose a wife from the place of his birth in Mesopotamia. When Nahor arrived at the well outside the city, he asked for God's help in his quest and even specified how he would know which girl it was. (If you want to know the code, look it up!) The account goes on, 'Before he had finished praying, Rebecca arrived ...' How's that for an answer to prayer?

When Joseph was asked if he could interpret Pharaoh's dream, he said, 'I cannot, Your Majesty, but God will give a favourable interpretation.' He did.

Shortly after the Israelites had been led from slavery in Egypt, they had three days without water, and when they found some, it was too bitter to drink. Moses prayed earnestly to the Lord, the Bible tells us, and the Lord showed him a piece of wood which he threw into the water. The water became fit to drink.

For many years, Hannah had been childless. She had to endure the humiliating taunts of Peninnah, her husband's other wife, who did have children. The situation was made worse because her husband, Elkanah, failed to understand her distress. She became depressed and couldn't eat. She was desperate. The chance of having a baby must have seemed remote, but she poured out her heart to God, not just for a baby but for a son. Soon after she returned home from their annual visit to the place of worship at Shiloh, she became pregnant. When her son was born (yes, it was a boy), she named him Samuel, because, she explained, 'I asked the LORD for him.'

When Solomon became king, he knew his task would not be easy (David was a hard act to follow), so he prayed for the wisdom to rule with justice and know the difference between good and evil. The result was that his reputation for wisdom spread far and wide.

Nehemiah, in exile in Persia and deeply saddened by news that the walls of Jerusalem were still in ruins long after most exiled Jews had returned home, prayed that God would give him the opportunity to ask his master, Emperor Artaxerxes, for help. He had to wait four months, but the opportunity came, and Artaxerxes could not have been more helpful. The walls were rebuilt.

When King Hezekiah of Judah received a letter from the Assyrian emperor threatening invasion, he took the letter to the temple and laid the problem before God. The Assyrian army was destroyed and there was no invasion.

In every case, God said yes.

In the New Testament, Cornelius prayed for guidance and promptly received it. Paul prayed for healing for Publius' father who had fever and dysentery; he recovered immediately. Peter's prayer even brought Tabitha back to life. In fact, the Bible is full of examples of people who called on God for safety, for victory, for healing, for guidance, for enlightenment, and received all they asked.

The Bible is by no means the only place to find examples of God saying yes. I can think of many instances in my own life when I was convinced that receiving was the result of asking, and so can most other Christians I know. Betty Pulkingham, in her book *Mustard Seeds*, tells how she was given the willpower to stop smoking. She had to use plenty of her own willpower as well, of course, but that is to be expected!

Malcolm and Christine Ford, who spend half of each year doing mission and aid work in Romania, tell of the pastor of a village church there who was anxious to evangelize other villages. He had people willing to do the work but no transport, so the church prayed for bicycles. What they did not know was that the bicycles, a gift from a church in Yeovil, were already on the way there!

One of the most striking examples of the direct and powerful activity of the Holy Spirit in response to prayer is the work of Jackie Pullinger in the old walled city of Hong Kong. In her books *Chasing the Dragon* and *Crack in the Wall*, she gives many instances of hardened drug addicts who were given immediate and lasting freedom from their craving for drugs as a result of prayer, no medication or other remedial measures at all being used.

Other situations in which people (admittedly

without proof but with good reason) are convinced that God intervened in response to prayer are the safe return of so many Allied troops from the beaches of Dunkirk in 1940 and the breaching of the Berlin Wall with the collapse of communism in 1989. Many more instances could be cited of God's kindly response to the requests of his children. The requests might have been big or small, wise or selfish; for guidance in times of doubt, for health in times of sickness, or for comfort in times of sorrow.

One question that perplexes many Christians is how we can be sure our prayers are effective when we don't know what would have happened if we hadn't prayed. As an agnostic would say, 'Because what you asked might have happened anyway, how can you prove that God had anything to do with it?' In terms of sheer logic, you can't prove it, but if you make prayer an important part of your Christian life, you soon realize beyond any doubt that the God who loves you and called you also cares for you. He has his hand on you for good, and delights in giving you many of the things you ask for.

In any case, if you ask for something and get it, it is only reasonable to assume that the answer is in response to the request, especially if it seems unlikely in human terms. Do you think Isaac or Joseph or Moses or Hannah or Solomon ever doubted that it was God who had given them what they asked?

Archbishop William Temple summed it up very well when he wrote, 'When I pray, coincidences happen, and when I do not, they don't.'

There is one sure way of *not* receiving the blessings

that God wants to give us, and that is by not asking for them. I have met many Christians who say, 'If God knows what we want, what is the point of telling him?' There's a great deal of point, and we only need to think about God as our Father to realize it.

Imagine yourself as a child, wanting things you know your father could provide and, what's more, quite confident that he is happy for you to have them. Would you just wait and hope? No, you would ask, partly because it would be the natural thing to do, and partly because you know your father would prefer you to. He would want you to share your feelings. He would like to know that his giving was in response to your asking. Most important of all, if you never asked for things you wanted, you would soon take them for granted and see no need to acknowledge the source or show any gratitude.

One of the Sunday-school prizes I had many years ago (for regular attendance, but not necessarily good conduct!) was a book about Wilfred Grenfell, who founded the Labrador Medical Mission in 1893 and was later knighted. I recall that he refused to pray for anything for himself. For others, by all means, but not himself. His reasoning was that he had committed his life to God, who knew his needs and could therefore be trusted to supply them. His discipline was to be greatly admired, but I can't quite go along with his thinking; he seems to have regarded God more as his employer than as his Father.

Asking is essential, then, because it establishes our dependence on God. It is not because he wants to make us feel indebted to him, but because we constantly need to recognize that without him we can do nothing. For this reason, God sometimes has to withhold blessings he is longing to give us. He once had to tell the kingdom of Judah, through the prophet Isaiah: 'I was ready to answer my people's prayers, but they did not pray.'

How necessary is it for us to have faith when we pray? It is vital, but we are still left with the question of what faith means in this context. It does not mean we must be 100% certain that what we ask will come to pass. It does mean that we must be certain that God is able to do what we ask if he, not we, knows it to be wise.

The point is that we must have faith in God, not in ourselves. This is best explained by examples.

Consider Elijah on Mount Carmel. He had challenged King Ahab to a big showdown between Baal and the one true God. Each side was to build an altar and call on their God to send fire from heaven to consume the sacrifice. The prophets of Baal tried first. No fire. Then it was Elijah's turn. There he stood on the mountain, confronted by the king, four hundred prophets of Baal, and a vast crowd of people, most of whom would have been glad to see him humiliated.

Elijah was about to pray for a miracle. If no fire came, he was finished. It wasn't like the toss of a coin, with a 50:50 chance. That fire *had* to come – everything depended on it. Yet such was the confidence Elijah had that he ordered the altar to be soaked with a dozen jars of water – and this was in a time of drought.

Then Elijah approached the altar and prayed. The fire came, as he knew it would. He knew because he had faith. He had faith because *God had given it to him.* Faith is one of the gifts of the Spirit. It is given by God to his servants so they can do his work.

Compare that with the prayer meeting in chapter 1. What did that group expect to happen as a result of their praying? Did George really think his prayer would have any effect on the government? Did Stella really believe that Ron would become accident-proof? And was Harold confident of receiving guidance as to his future?

Yes, George should; no, Stella shouldn't; and yes, Harold should be. We'll come back to Stella in the next chapter, but look now at the other two situations in turn.

What is the point of praying for the government (whether national or local), the Royal Family, or any others in authority? What difference will my little prayer make? The apostle Paul touched on this question in his letter to the Romans. He was concerned with obeying the state authorities. They rule only under God and therefore should be supported by all God-fearing people.

You may wish to question whether we in the United Kingdom are still ruled by our Sovereign Lady, Queen Elizabeth, with the assistance of Parliament, as the 1662 *Book of Common Prayer* has it, but the Church of England does firmly recognize the need to pray for people in high office. Many free churches, on the other hand, ignore this matter completely. Notice that we should pray for *all* those in positions of authority, not just for the government and the Royal Family. It is right to support in prayer all those who carry burdens of responsibility – bishops, trades-union leaders, head teachers, company directors and so on. That is not to say that we use our prayers to try to control their decisions; what we pray is that God will influence their decisions. It is because we are wanting God's will to be done and not ours that we can be confident that God will do as we ask.

We should never take the view that we are insignificant citizens and therefore our prayers carry little weight. Prayer doesn't work like that. We certainly hope that many others are offering similar prayers, but that need not concern us; prayers are not like opinion polls. All that matters is that we faithfully help people to carry heavy responsibilities by asking God to guide them by his Holy Spirit. He will do so, but whether we will be able to see that he has, or how he has, is another matter.

Asking for guidance is another aspect of prayer in which we can be sure our Father will never refuse us. The one thing he wants more than anything is that we should be following his direction, so there is no way he will fail to give it. The big problem here is that we don't always recognize the guidance when it's given. And sometimes we don't really want God's guidance at all; what we want is his endorsement of *our* plans.

I recall a young Christian who would stand up in church at regular intervals and ask everyone to pray for her because she knew that God was calling her to full-time Christian work but had not revealed what it was. I'm sure she was being absolutely sincere. She had a comfortable home and a well-paid job. Thirty years later, she still has. It's no use asking questions if we don't listen for answers.

The only way to receive guidance from God is to take whatever action *we* can and go on trusting that God will be directing us as we do. The direction may take the form of preventing us from doing something we are sure is right, which can be extremely frustrating. It may also take a long time, which can be most discouraging. We have to learn to trust and go on trusting. That can be a difficult thing to do, but God can only use people who are prepared to trust him completely in every situation.

So if Harold is going to do nothing while he listens for a voice or waits for a vision, he may wait a long time. God works through our thought and action, not outside it. Harold must therefore consider the avenues of full-time service. It could be the ministry, the mission field – or the police. God doesn't want all his front-line troops in church-based situations. It could be that God wants him to stay in his present job and be a Christian sales rep or teacher or whatever he is.

Having considered the possibilities, he must make whatever first approaches seem right. That may mean obtaining information from a missionary society or theological college, Voluntary Service Overseas, TEAR Fund or any other appropriate source. He must also go on discussing his call with Christian friends. They may be able to see his talents (and shortcomings) better than he can himself, and their advice – so long as they are completely honest, as they should be – will be vital. What Harold must never do is think that God hasn't heard or doesn't care. That cannot be true, because God's whole nature is love.

Prayers for guidance should not be restricted to matters of Christian service, whether full-time or part-time. We should all ask God to guide us in every major decision we have to make. Who we marry, where we live, what job we do, how we handle our money or spend our holidays – in all these and many other aspects of our lives we should be asking God by his Spirit to control our thinking and our decisions.

As with Harold, we may experience the same problems of being unsure about the guidance we receive. When we read the Bible, it all seems so easy. We are given the exact words that God used in speaking to his servants. (It's strange that the Bible should use only direct speech, even when recording events that took place many generations earlier.) In fact, we can be sure that those who served God, whether as prophets, apostles or whatever, faced the same difficulties as we do in hearing God's voice. They knew doubt and discouragement, but went on trusting and obeying until the message became clear.

The best way to understand guidance is to use the analogy of the telephone. We can be absolutely certain that God always hears and answers, but we cannot always get the message clearly or quickly because of interference on the line. That distortion is our sinfulness or selfishness. But the more we listen, and the more we get others to listen with us and for us, the more sure we will become that God is guiding our way.

Christians are often encouraged to keep a record of 'answered prayers'. In some ways this is a good idea. It enables us to look back with praise to God for his guidance and gratitude to him for his goodness. But the big snag with this idea is the implication that the only acceptable answer to prayer is to get what we ask for. That is not so. Whatever response God makes to our prayers must be right, because he is a wise and loving Father.

Isn't it good to know that there will be many occasions when God will smile and say yes?

Chapter 7

The second answer: No

What would you think of a father who gave his three-year-old son a scalpel to sharpen a pencil with? It wouldn't do the scalpel much good, but what is far more important is that it would put the boy in serious danger or temptation. It is something no father would do, simply because he would know better. The boy might ask, and even plead, but the answer would be no.

You may think there is no parallel between that and God refusing our prayer requests. We wouldn't ask for anything so stupid or dangerous. Wouldn't we? There are many occasions when we are quite convinced that what we ask must be in accordance with God's purposes, but if only we knew what God knows, we would know better than to ask.

Since we never will know all that God knows, and often couldn't understand it if we did, we must expect there to be times when we ask for something in prayer and God has to say no. Jean Ingelow once wrote, 'I have lived to thank God that all my prayers have not been answered.' That has certainly been true of my own life too. I can think of things I once wanted quite desperately, and therefore prayed for earnestly, but which, I now realize, would have done me no good at all. My heavenly Father knew better and said no.

There must have been many other occasions when I never did discover why God said no; it has been a matter of learning to trust his love and wisdom without asking questions.

A well-known refusal of a prayer request in the Bible concerns the apostle Paul's 'thorn in the flesh'. Writing to the Christians in Corinth, Paul says he had asked God three times to remove this problem, to no avail. We cannot be quite sure what the problem was, and it has been a matter of much speculation by Bible scholars. There are several possibilities.

We often describe a person who is a continual nuisance as a 'thorn in the flesh', and Paul certainly had enemies of Christ who persecuted him and fellow Christians who opposed him; and he did describe his 'thorn' as 'a messenger from Satan'. This suggests it might have been a person who was hindering his work. But surely it was not in Paul's nature to ask God to eliminate hindrances in this way.

It could have been a physical deformity. In the apocryphal *Acts of Paul and Thecla*, we have a description of Paul as 'a man of little stature, thin-haired upon the head, crooked in the legs, of good state of body, with eyebrows meeting, and nose somewhat hooked'. Not very flattering! Not a very likely explanation either.

Or it could have been a personality defect. Paul could be sharp-tongued at times, as we can see from his uncharacteristic outbursts in Galatians 5:12 and 1 Corinthians 16:22, and the fact that he had a heated disagreement with Barnabas. But I think that is very unlikely, as at least one modern translation (Good News Bible) talks of a 'painful *physical* ailment'. Three of these have been suggested.

Bishop Lightfoot thought it might be epilepsy. (If so, it is something he had in common with Julius Caesar, Muhammad, King Alfred and the Russian Tsar, Peter the Great.) A feature of epilepsy, however, is that over a long period it causes mental deterioration. There was certainly no sign of that with Paul.

Dean Farrar and others argued that it was poor eyesight, on the grounds that Saul (as he was then) was temporarily blinded on the Damascus road, that in his letter to the Galatians he drew attention to his large handwriting, and that in the same letter he commented on their willingness to give him their own eyes if they could.

Others, including William Barclay, reckon it was malaria. It is suggested that he contracted the disease on his first missionary journey in the low-lying area near Perga in southern Asia Minor, which is why he went north into Galatia.

Whatever it was, it was recurrent, painful, humiliating and a hindrance to his work. No wonder he asked God to take it away. He must have said, as any of us probably would, 'This *cannot* be God's will.' (He may well have thought the same at times about being in prison when he wanted to be preaching.) So he asked

God for healing. Nothing happened. He asked again. Still nothing happened.

After the third 'no', I would suggest that he thought like this. If God says no, there must be a reason, whether I can see it or not. If God won't remove the problem, he must mean me to have it. If he means it, it must be right. If it's right, it must be good. Once he reached this point, he was able to see that the purpose was to keep him humble, from 'being puffed up with pride' as the Bible says.

Paul was a clever man; had there been doctors of divinity in his day, he would have been one (unlike Peter, who would probably have failed his GCSE!). He was important, and, for all his setbacks, had an enormously successful ministry. Pride could be a serious problem in a situation like that. It is a measure of Paul's greatness that he could see that. So he stopped asking. He accepted that God knew what he was doing. How often do we?

An even better-known example of God saying no relates to the prayer of Jesus in Gethsemane just before his arrest. The Bible makes it plain that Jesus was in extreme agony of spirit; he was at the absolute limit of what anyone could face. He knew exactly what lay just ahead of him – betrayal by one of his close friends, denial by another, and desertion by the rest. There would be a mockery of a trial, whipping, spitting and ridicule, followed by a slow and barbaric death. Knowing all that, he asked God (his Father, remember) if there were any other way by which he could carry out his task of redemption without having to go through the horror of crucifixion.

He asked, but immediately added those words of humility and submission, 'Yet not what I want, but what you want.' These words, spoken or unspoken, must always be built in to every prayer. In this case God had to say no because there was no other way for us to be saved; the whole success of Jesus' rescue mission depended on his accepting the punishment for our sins on the cross.

Teaching us humility is only one of many reasons that God may have for saying no. We may have to suffer so that we can minister to others who face a similar situation. God may have plans for us that we are not yet ready to receive, and giving us what we ask would get in the way of them. It may well be that some of God's no's cannot make sense to us during this life.

Another reason why we sometimes feel that God is denying us things we ask is that we are prone to confuse *needs* with *wants*. In our acquisitive society, we see it happening all around us, and few of us are immune to self-indulgence. God promises us daily bread, but we are not satisfied with that; we expect, as of right, a more attractive diet! And we usually get it. In a world in which so many are malnourished, we need to be reminded to trust our heavenly Father to provide what we need, and thank him on the many occasions when he gives us so much more.

The first Christians were no strangers to prayer requests being refused. How earnestly they must have prayed for Stephen as he witnessed before the Council; but he was still martyred. They would not have realized that Stephen's death was the beginning of Saul's conversion, nor that his courage was to inspire many more to hold their lives cheap for the sake of the gospel.

In the same way, many thousands of prayers must have been offered for relief from the successive waves of persecution that were suffered by the church over the next three centuries, but the persecution went on. It must have caused great suffering and distress but through it the church grew and spread.

Back to our typical prayer meeting. Did Stella really expect her prayer to guarantee a safe flight for Ron? When the aircraft touched down safely, would it have been due to her praying, the collective skills of airline and aviation authorities personnel, or God's intervention? Suppose the aircraft had crashed. If Ron had walked from the wreckage completely unharmed, that would presumably have been a triumph for prayer. But would it? Would it not have mattered that other wives had been widowed and many lives shattered?

Whenever we pray, we must always be sure of just what we are asking for, and why. Do we really expect, or even want, Christians to be shielded from the risks that others face? Our faith should enable us to confront danger and loss bravely and go through times of adversity calmly, not lead us to expect to be kept from them. God loves all his children and would like to keep them all from harm and danger, but it is our responsibility to make travel as safe as we can, not his. If we (humankind, that is) choose to benefit from technology, we must all accept the risks that go with it. Stella has no right to expect special protection for her husband, or that his flight should be safe because he is on it.

That is not to say that she should not share her fears with God, praying that he will give her a sense of trust and an assurance that both she and Ron are in his hands wherever they are and whatever happens. And of course, the others praying with her should share in that concern; that's fellowship.

There is a further reason why God sometimes has to say no, and that is guilt. This is the one we often overlook, either because we prefer not to think about it or because we are unaware of it.

Let's give an example. A woman is attracted to a man she works with. It soon becomes clear that the attraction is mutual. It is easy to see how it can happen. Everyone likes to have attention paid to them, and flattery readily evokes a response.

So the woman, almost without noticing it at first, dresses attractively when that man is around, and is always helpful to him. He is polite and considerate in return. Meanwhile, his wife is at home coping with young children, the hoovering and the ironing, and when he gets home at night she is, let us say, not at her brightest. Eventually, the two colleagues start looking for ways to meet outside office hours. The scenario is all too familiar. The affair develops so gradually that by the time they realize the full extent of their feelings for each other, the chances of retreat are becoming slim indeed.

The woman is a Christian. She knows, as her married colleague knows, that what they are doing is wrong. Nevertheless, she goes to church every Sunday as usual. But what is happening to her prayer life? It is becoming ineffectual. This is not because God is trying to punish her, but simply because her sin has created a barrier between her and God. She *cannot* pray in the Spirit, or 'in the name of Jesus'. The guilt, whether acknowledged, suppressed or excused, has broken the spiritual contact.

The affair, the possibility of which she should have been aware of and avoided long before, must be ended if her peace with God is to be restored.

So when God says no to our requests, it is either because he knows better than we do or because he has something to teach us. God's refusals cannot be failures, because he always wants our highest good.

Chapter 8

The third answer: Wait

Most of us are impatient by nature. When we want something, we want it now. We joke about the prayer that says, 'Lord, teach me patience, and hurry up about it', but it's very true to life. It is not easy to accept that God's work must be done in God's time. We have one life on earth and are always in a hurry to see results; God plans for eternity. That means that God often has to delay giving us what we ask until the moment he knows is right. As Girolamo Savonarola, the fifteenth-century reforming monk and farmer, said, 'Never think that God's delays are God's denials.'

The Jews prayed for their promised Messiah for centuries before Jesus came. God had not forgotten or stopped listening. He knew exactly what he was going to do, and when he was going to do it, as the apostle Paul pointed out in his letter to the Galatians. It is very sad that when Jesus did come, most Jews failed to recognize him as their Messiah because they could think only in terms of a military or political saviour.

There are two other biblical prayers that still await fulfilment. The first is the prayer of Jesus for the unity of his church. Just before his arrest and crucifixion, he prayed that his followers might all 'be one just as you and I are one'. Yet two millennia later, the church is still torn by division.

We know that since God is our Father, it must follow that we are all brothers and sisters, and should love and accept each other as part of one family. But we don't. We keep apart, in our own churches and denominations. Or we insist that all denominations are astray from the Bible, not realizing that that very attitude creates another denomination, however small. We claim to have all the truth and refute the claims of others, or even deny they are Christians at all. We make token gestures of co-operation, in between periods of criticism and competition. One day, in the fulfilment of the kingdom, our Saviour's prayer will become a reality, but in the meantime it calls for a great deal of penitence, love and action on our part. How can we ever complain of having to wait when our Father is still waiting for us to love our fellow Christians, let alone our enemies?

The other unfulfilled biblical prayer, found at the conclusion of Revelation, is the apostle John's prayer that the second coming might not be delayed: 'Come Lord Jesus.' The expectation of the whole of the early church was that the return of Jesus was imminent, and as John was writing at a time of fierce persecution, it was understandable that he should end his apocalypse with such a plea. But Jesus didn't return, and still hasn't.

The apostle Peter, in his second letter, had a word for those who were becoming impatient – and that was around AD 67! He suggested that the return of Jesus was being mercifully delayed to give people the opportunity to respond to the gospel. If that were true then, perhaps it is still true; if so, what does it say to us about missionary endeavour?

One reason for what seems to be a long-delayed response to prayer can be that we are waiting for God to act when in fact he is waiting for us. We feel that what we are praying for is entirely dependent on some action by the Holy Spirit and that that action is not forthcoming. In our self-centredness we fail to realize what we have to do.

Another reason is that we are never quite sure whether long-running prayer topics indicate faithfulness in prayer or failure to trust. We recall that Jesus once told his disciples a parable to teach them 'that they should always pray and never become discouraged', and the apostle Paul encouraged the Christians in Colossae to 'be persistent in prayer'. (Recalling the time that Terry Waite spent in captivity as a hostage makes us realize just how much persistence must have been needed by the many people who prayed in earnest for his release. The waiting must have been agonizing for those close to him, but he *was* freed. The outcome could have been very different.)

Do these exhortations mean we never 'close a file' on a prayer request, but go on asking and never give in? No, there are times when we persevere and others when we take no for an answer. There are also times when we put the matter on hold, as it were. That is, we stop praying for a while and leave the issue in God's hands. But how do we know which is which?

There is no simple answer, but some general guidance can be given. First, when we reach the point where it seems that we are praying in vain, we should ask ourselves why. It may be that the answer will be quite plain as soon as we look for it. Failing that, ask God why. Maybe that's just what he's waiting for, but we are too keen on getting our request granted to ask him.

Secondly, if the prayer is for yourself (your health, for example), be more ready to stop asking than if it is a request for the benefit of somebody else. If it were for your own benefit, you may have been showing a lack of trust, asking God for something instead of accepting the promises that Jesus talked about in the Sermon on the Mount (see the last part of Matthew 6). If you have someone else in mind, perseverance may be more appropriate, although you may still, on reflection, decide that having made your request, you will leave the outcome in God's hands.

Thirdly, if the prayer is for a material blessing (like a better job), ask yourself whether you should have been praying for it at all. If it is for a spiritual blessing (for guidance, power to overcome a particular temptation, understanding of Scripture, and so on), be ready to go on praying until your needs are met; or unless you reach a point at which you are quite sure God is leading you to stop. This is one of those cases where sharing your concern with one or more Christians can be of great benefit.

One of the commonest examples of a long-running prayer request is the prayer that a child, or other relative or close friend, might make a Christian commitment. It is a poor Christian parent who fails to pray for something as important as that. In the nature of things, that praying can go on for a very long time. When, if ever, should we decide not to continue? I suggest there can be two possible reasons for desisting.

The first is that we find it impossible to pray with sincerity because it has become a routine with little meaning. The request is as real as ever but it has become hard to feel it can ever happen. It may be that as soon as you admit that to yourself, the urge to pray returns; but if it doesn't, why not keep praying, but less often, say, once a week or once a month instead of daily?

The other reason can be that your praying is actually tending to spoil your relationship. That is, your enthusiasm to see that person saved, good and right as it is, is hindering you from accepting and loving your relative as he or she is ***now***, as we are meant to do.

As an evangelical Christian, I believe that no-one can be saved unless the Holy Spirit first works in that life, convicting of sin and convincing of the truth of Jesus as Saviour. That is what we pray for, but we have to recognize that, for reasons we will never understand (in this life, that is), the Spirit works in some lives but not in others – or that is how it appears to us. Of course, there is always the possibility that we are praying when we should be witnessing, and that is something we will consider under the fourth answer to prayer.

We have already seen in our typical prayer meeting that Harold may need to learn patience and trust as he prays for guidance. He may think, 'Surely, if God wants me to serve him, he should have opened a door by now; perhaps I was mistaken in my call.' Yes, Harold, perhaps you were; it does happen. On the other hand, perhaps you weren't. This is where sharing your feelings with other Christians is so valuable. As you discuss and pray about the situation together, you will learn whether you should re-think your future or go on waiting and trusting.

I have some friends, a young couple, who have recently been in exactly this position. They became convinced that God wanted them in full-time Christian service. They prayed, and others prayed with them and for them. They examined various possibilities of service, at home or abroad, and were quite open to any leading. It seemed right to go to a Bible college, so they left well-paid jobs and went. After two years training, they still did not know their future. For months they searched, applied for posts, went for interviews, accepted preaching engagements – and went on praying.

Their patience and trust in God's guidance were severely tested, but in spite of understandable moments of discouragement and frustration, they remained convinced that God had a work for them and was preparing them for it. Then they heard of a part-time course at a theological college which was combined with lay ministry at a church. They applied, and were accepted. At the end of the course the husband was ordained, and then they had to find a church. The time lapse between call and settlement was seven years.

And just in case you think that timescale indicated any lack of ability on their part, let me say that their lay ministry over this period was greatly valued, by their home church and by others.

More recently, a man I know applied to become a pilot with the Missionary Aviation Fellowship. He was already a fully qualified pilot, and was eager to get on with the task to which he had been called. But there were all sorts of delays; including the lack of places on an essential course for flying in jungle terrain. Now, he and his wife are in Africa at last, but they had to learn patience before they got there.

Derek may feel equally despondent as he brings his need of a job to God. When we are out of work, each week seems like ten. We get frustrated by inactivity and concerned about paying the bills, and all this on top of the feeling of being unwanted that goes with redundancy. When the days of unsuccessful job-hunting drag on and on, it is all too easy to become discouraged and to begin to doubt God's providence. This is one of those times when the prayer and practical support of a caring Christian fellowship are of real value.

Clinical depression is another situation in which we must be prepared to persevere in prayer. We see or hear of instantaneous healings, and cannot see why all illness, mental and physical, should not be healed that way. When we think like that, we are falling into the basic human sin of pride – expecting God to conform to *our* wishes.

We must learn that in this, as in every situation, God is neither idle nor careless, but knows, cares, and will provide for all our needs if we trust him. (Notice that all our *wants* are not necessarily included.) What we may have to realize is that learning to wait on God and go on trusting him may itself be a part of the answer to our prayer.

Chapter 9

The fourth answer: DIY

If you asked your human father to do something you were quite capable of doing for yourself, what would he be most likely to say? Yes, 'Do it yourself!' Not because he is lazy or unhelpful but because it is in your interests as well as his that you should do whatever you can. If you need help, he will give it. If you don't know how to do it, he will show you. But a helpless child and an over-indulgent father make a pitiful pair.

In the same way, our heavenly Father teaches us and helps us, but wants us to be capable, willing and hard-working. The big difference between God and human fathers is that once we begin any task God wants us to do, he doesn't stand back and let us get on with it but works through us to achieve his purposes. Few things in this life are as satisfying as knowing that we are channels through which God's power is at work. It is easy to see the effect this must have on our prayers. We must never ask God to do what we should be doing, although we will often be asking him for guidance in how we do it, and perhaps for the grace, the strength or the perseverance to carry it out.

Our typical prayer meeting was full of examples of prayers that should have been replaced by action, or at least supplemented by it. The first request was for Mrs Hodges, who'd had a fall. It was right to pray for her. But did that group stop to consider ways in which they could be of practical help? They may have suggested that she should have the church flowers on the following Sunday, but did they make arrangements for people to visit her in hospital? Time crawls slowly when you are in a hospital bed, and visits make a big difference. Did anyone ask whether she had a dog to take out, a cat to feed? People worry about things like that. Or did they find out whether she needed any washing done? If not, they should have done, because then they could have been part of the answer to their own prayers. If they did, full marks.

Then they prayed for the minister, as of course they should. I hope they joined their prayers to those of the minister himself, asking that the Holy Spirit would fill his mind and heart as he led people in worship, expounded the Bible, and went about his work of visiting and counselling. But did they also make a mental note to give him a word of encouragement, or perhaps invite him and his wife to a meal?

Praying for Helen, the missionary in Brazil, provided even more opportunities for them to answer their own prayers. They could decide to write to her and perhaps send her some magazines; no, they *don't* always have to be religious ones! If the church had the necessary equipment, they could arrange for a tape of one of the services to be made, adding some personal greetings from members of the congregation.

Perhaps there was not much they could do to advise or assist Derek in his search for a new job, except that they should be aware that he might have time on his hands and might welcome the occasional social visit or invitation.

If their practical help for Derek was limited, there was certainly plenty they could do for Harold. They could, and should, have had a real part to play in his search for guidance about full-time Christian service. Much of the answer to Harold's request would come in the form of advice and suggestions from fellow Christians. They should therefore be ready to give time to think and talk with him as well as pray with him.

Then there was Mary and her migraines. Was her problem spiritual, medical or just a part of her personality? We will look at that again when we consider prayers for healing, but healing and counselling aside, Mary had a problem that could almost certainly be alleviated by friendship and understanding; and friendship can be time-consuming.

The request to pray for Africa reminds us that Christians need to keep well informed on what is happening in the world if we are to pray intelligently for God's intervention in its many economic, political and social problems. That may not be easy. It is true that we are bombarded with news bulletins and there are plenty of newspapers, but they don't always tell us what we need to know. Most newspapers are politically biased, and both they and TV and radio select or colour the items they report to provide excitement and opinion as well as factual information.

Even when we can be confident that the news is presented accurately and objectively, we still may not be given the background knowledge that is essential if we are to understand the situation fully. Wide and careful reading, viewing and listening are therefore necessary, with Christian magazines often giving information that the secular media sometimes fail to provide.

One valuable source of background information to stimulate and guide our prayer for world mission is the book *Operation World*, published by OM Publishing in the UK and OM LIT in the USA, who also issue sets of eighty prayer cards, each card describing the situation and needs in a particular country.

Praying for revival, whether in general terms or for some particular evangelistic initiative, is another situation where prayer and action must go hand in hand. None would dispute the statement that there can be no revival without prayer; history has clearly shown that every great revival was born of, and nurtured by, prayer. It is the work of the Holy Spirit, not us, to bring people to an understanding of the gospel and their need for salvation, so we need to ask, and go on asking, for that activity.

But prayer alone is not enough. It is no use saying there is nothing we can do but pray. Jesus, in what we call the Great Commission, made it very plain that the major task of his church was to be preaching, teaching, and baptizing. If we don't do this, it won't be done. As

A. W. Pink pointed out, the church that does not evangelize will fossilize.

Because evangelism, whether in our own locality or through foreign missions, must always be high on our agenda, every prayer meeting should be a briefing session for the battle to which every Christian is called. Your part in that battle may take place in a pulpit, on somebody's doorstep, over the garden fence, in the works canteen, or in your child's bedroom, and prayer provides the ammunition for the fight.

When William Carey, in 1792, began to stir the conscience of British churches to the need for overseas missionary endeavour, he was told, 'Sit down, young man! When God chooses to convert the heathen, he will do it without your help or mine.' We now know that God won't do it without our help. At least, most of us do. There are still some people who think that the doctrine of election lets them off the hook: 'If God is going to save them anyway, I don't need to do anything.' But if God has decided to save someone, how do you know that he hasn't also decided that you will be his mouthpiece?

Preaching or teaching makes the same demand for prayer to be wedded to action as does evangelism. Before we prepare a sermon or a Sunday-school lesson, we must ask the Holy Spirit to feed our minds and also open the minds of those who will hear us. At the same time, we must make the effort to study and prepare. Spiritual and intellectual resources depend on each other.

While on the topic of evangelism, we should note that *living* the gospel always takes precedence over *telling* it. The usual set of activities associated with spreading the gospel (missions, door-knocking, inviting to church, distributing Christian literature) will all be compromised if the quality of our lives is substandard. People will always watch us more closely than they will listen to us. St Francis of Assisi put it well when he said: 'Preach the gospel at all times. If necessary, use words.'

Would you agree to Linda's request to pray that Fiona does well in her GCSEs? I hope not. This is a clear case where we have no right to ask God to act. If Fiona has worked hard, she will get grades that do justice to her ability; if she hasn't, she doesn't deserve them. If God arranged for Fiona's results to be improved because Linda prayed for her, it would be quite unfair on her schoolmates, who had no such advantage. In a way, it would also be unfair on Fiona, because if she did well she would no longer deserve the credit for it. We know, however, how stressful exams can be, and there is every reason to pray that Fiona will be relaxed and able to think clearly. That is very different from asking God to manipulate exam results.

A similar situation arises with Sylvia's request for prayer that she might pass her driving test. We can all understand her eagerness to pass, and it may be that it would make a world of difference to her – being able to get a better job, for example, or making more frequent visits to an elderly relative. No matter. Passing must be on the ability to drive and nothing else. How would you feel if you had passed a test because you had prayed about it, and then caused an accident in which someone was killed because you did not really have the ability to drive alone? Here again, prayer for freedom from debilitating nerves is commendable; prayer to influence the examiner is not.

Ruth's desire that Wayne will get the job he is being interviewed for is equally understandable. What sort of mother would she be if she didn't care? But the point is that the job should go to the best candidate, not the one who bends God's ear. Of course, if Wayne gets the job, it would be absolutely right to thank God for the outcome – and be pleased that he did it on merit, not on divine nepotism.

God longs to work through us to achieve his purposes, so we should always be offering ourselves to be used by him; but if we find ourselves asking him to do what should properly depend on our ability or effort (as from time to time most of us do), we must expect the answer to be, 'Do it yourself.' That is still true when we are asking God's help for someone else.

The apostle James, in his open letter to 'all God's people', stressed the need for our faith to be demonstrated by action. He pointed out that faith that does not result in practical activity is not true faith. He demolished the idea of some people being spiritual while others are practical. This reminds us that there are many occasions when we can pray with our purse or wallet. We get plenty of mail from charities, aid agencies and missionary societies. They all hope that we will take enough interest in their work to pray for it as well as give to it. Within the limits of our time, so we should. But always remember that a cheque book *can* have a place in the work of the kingdom.

There are many other examples in the Bible of prayer being inextricably linked to action. We know that the apostle Paul prayed long and earnestly for people and churches for whom he felt a responsibility; but how much poorer would the infant church have been if he had *only* prayed? Even more to the point, suppose Jesus had prayed for us *instead* of taking the way of the cross.

Chapter 10

The fifth answer: MYOB!

Mind your own business! When we use that phrase, it is intended as a brush-off and is regarded as rather rude, or at least ungracious. We all know that God is neither. I am using it as a courteous but firm statement that in our prayers there are some questions that should not be asked and some requests that should not be made.

God sometimes has to say to us, 'That's my affair – not yours.' In our humanity, there are some things we are not meant to know, if only because our finite (perhaps 'puny' is a better word) minds could not understand them. One very obvious example is praying for recovery from a terminal illness. We shall look at the question of praying for healing in the next chapter, but prayer for healing which means asking for prolongation of life is a special case.

It's a natural enough thing to do. Our human minds are so designed that we cling to life, both our own and that of our loved ones. We hate the thought of parting. There are exceptions to this, and where a person is obviously senile or in great pain, most Christians (and non-Christians for that matter) would be more likely to pray for a peaceful end and freedom from suffering.

Yet still there are those who will pray for healing as though no other outcome can ever really be acceptable. They will pray most fervently for recovery for patients in the advanced stages of a terminal, and possibly painful, illness. In such a situation, we need to ask ourselves, 'What if the answer to my prayer is to give me what I ask? Might the result be just a few years of weakness and constant pain before the same illness returns?'

In this connection, I can recount an incident from my own experience. Many years ago, my mother was suffering from cancer. She was in a hostel run by a religious order and not expected to live more than a few days. It was a Sunday and I asked my minister to pray for her in the evening service – which he did, with evident sincerity, as of course I did myself. The next morning my mother was so much better that she discharged herself from the hostel. Recently widowed, she then lived a somewhat lonely and joyless life in a basement flat at some distance from her family, until the cancer reasserted itself. This time, she had a much longer and more painful spell in hospital before she died.

Was I right to pray for her recovery? It seemed the only right thing to do at the time; now I wonder if it was not more selfish than loving.

It can be argued that the prayers had no effect at all;

that what happened would have happened anyway. After all, it must be true of all our prayers that we cannot know categorically whether they are effective or not, because we can never be sure what would have happened if we had not prayed. Nor can we know what outcome other people may have been praying for.

In practice, though, if we ask God for something we could rationally expect to happen, and it does happen, then it is reasonable to assume that our prayers have been effective. More to the point, prayer being a spiritual exercise and not a pragmatic one, we can expect the same Holy Spirit who guides us in praying also to show us what happens as a result of those prayers.

I certainly felt that what happened to my mother was an answer to prayer. At the time, I rejoiced. Looking back, I'm not so sure. One day, I'll know.

This same problem occurred in our typical prayer meeting, where Jean requested prayer because her colleague's uncle had suffered a heart attack. We often pray for recovery just because it seems the natural thing to do, but God in his wisdom may have kinder plans. It must be right, however, to pray for comfort, peace of mind, and the assurance that God cares, not only for the uncle but for all his family. It is important, by the way, that Jean should tell her colleague about these prayers, both to assure them of her concern and as a witness to her belief.

We can face the same problem in reverse – praying that God will terminate a life that is beset by weakness and pain. For many, it is natural to want the patient to be released from suffering, especially if we can see little or no chance that he or she is ever likely to recover.

But what if God can see the chance that we can't? And can we always be completely sure of our motives, when it is so easy to cover our desire to be rid of a liability with a smoke-screen of compassion?

We should by all means lay our burdens of concern on the Lord, but let him decide when to take to himself the life he created. If he seems to delay, be sure he has his reasons. One of them may be the need to refine your character, whatever the cost.

Another no-go area which Christians all too often enter is trying to know the future. We are all familiar with Jehovah's Witnesses on our doorstep pointing out, with detailed reasons, why our Lord's second coming is near.

(Digressing for a moment, I hope you never send JWs away rudely. Even if it is at an inconvenient moment, as most unexpected calls are, please find time to tell them what *you* believe and why. Don't argue, and don't get hooked into their rehearsed dialogue, but share with them, simply and sincerely, your joy and freedom in being saved.)

JWs are not the only people who claim a sure knowledge of the imminence of Christ's return; there are some in the mainstream of Christianity who do it. How do they know? Primarily, they would regard the Bible as their authority, quoting Matthew 24 and 25 and Revelation in particular.

It is indeed true that the Bible is the Christian's prime source of truth and guidance. That is not to say that we can use it as a technician uses a manual. It is not as easy as that. The Bible is unique in that the truth and guidance it contains are revealed *through* God's

Word *by* God's Spirit. In the words of William Cowper, in one of the *Olney Hymns*, published in 1779, 'The Spirit breathes upon the Word, And brings the truth to sight.' While the meaning of many passages is clear enough and most people agree on them, we know only too well that others are capable of widely differing interpretations, some of which have been responsible for deep divisions within the church for centuries.

It is certainly true that God enlightens our minds through prayer, but the mere fact that two people can read the same biblical passage and claim to have been given quite different interpretations of its meaning, shows us that, as with the party game 'Chinese whispers', it is all too easy for us to mis-hear the messages we receive. So when we say 'the Bible says that ...' or 'The Holy Spirit told me that ...', we must accept that our understanding may not be the only one.

Where Christ's return to earth is concerned, however, it is hard to see how anyone can claim any revelation about the timing of that event when the Bible clearly states that we are to remain in ignorance. Even Jesus himself didn't know when he would return. Matthew 24:36 says, 'No one knows, however, when that day and hour will come – neither the angels in heaven nor the Son; the Father alone knows.' Similar words are found in Mark's gospel.

It is not surprising that in eschatology (the doctrine of the last things) our mortal minds can easily get out of their depth. The Bible ends, as it begins, in mystery. We are told all the truth we need to know but not the details that would be beyond our understanding.

It is in the mercy of God that the future, whether of

individuals or the whole of humankind, remains in his hands. Just ponder for a moment some of the awful situations we would face if we knew what awaited us. If we could see the future, we would be quite unable to cope with the present.

When Mary Brainard wrote the hymn that begins, 'I know not what awaits me, God kindly veils mine eyes', she knew the importance of trusting God. That's why the last verse reads:

So on I go not knowing, I would not if I might;
I'd rather walk in the dark with God than go
alone in the light;
I'd rather walk by faith with him than go alone by
sight.

We all have to face hard times during our lives. When they come, we can cope with them – with a little help from our friends, and the strength of the Holy Spirit. If we knew what was coming, we would most likely crack up. Suppose, for example, you knew that your house was going to burn down next week. (No, you wouldn't be able to prevent it if you knew that it *was* going to burn down.)

Imagine how we would feel and what we would do if we knew that Christ was coming again next week. More to the point, supposing we knew that he *wasn't* coming for another thousand years. There is nothing we like better than an excuse for delaying the work of mission that needs to be done, and Satan knows it only too well. We have the past to learn from and the present to use; let's leave the future to God.

Something that has been the subject of countless prayers through the ages is the weather. Usually it has been a case of individuals or groups asking for fine weather on special occasions – a church fête, for example, or, as in the typical prayer meeting in chapter 1, for a junior-church or Sunday-school anniversary. At other times, it has been a matter of concerted action by many people, as when they are called to pray for rain in times of drought.

Initially it may seem a reasonable request. A fine day can make a world of difference to a fête or outing, and, since God is in charge of the weather, why not ask him to help? A little thought will show there are very good reasons why not.

First, it may be that while you are praying for sunshine, local farmers are praying for much-needed rain. For that reason alone, it would make sense to leave God to control the weather, to accept that he knows best and all his ways are wise.

Conflicting or competing prayers are not the only problem. Even if we could all agree on what to ask for, our prayers for the weather we would *like* would undoubtedly outnumber prayers for the weather we *need*; and that assumes we would know what we need, which is doubtful. Again, it is better to let God decide. As somebody once said, 'If I had God's power for one day, what changes I would make! But if I had his wisdom too, I'd leave things as they are.'

There is yet another reason for avoiding the selfish practice of persuading God to make the weather suit our purposes. The weather is not controlled on an hour-to-hour basis, as though God is sitting in some heavenly control centre deploying wind, sun and rain as he thinks fit. It may seem like that at times (especially in Britain), but a glance at any of the newspaper or TV weather charts makes it clear that every shower or sunny interval is caused by a complex interaction of winds, tides and temperatures (each governed by immutable scientific laws) as they relate to geographical features. Every line and arrow on those charts is determined by the lines and arrows that were on the previous one, and which change from moment to moment.

Of course, God can, if he chooses, intervene at any time to affect the normal operation of his own laws, but we have to understand that praying for a fine day is asking for a miracle, not the granting of a simple favour from an indulgent Father. Is that what we really want, especially when our satisfaction may adversely affect many other people?

It is of course right and proper that any wishes we may have about the weather, be it for a fine day for a wedding or for heavy rain to save wilting crops, should be shared with our Father in our prayer times, but we should still accept the discipline of never asking God to satisfy our personal desires without regard for the wider implications that only God is in a position to appreciate.

Much depends on the attitude with which we begin our prayers. Do we focus on God's wisdom and perfect knowledge, or do we see him as a provider first and foremost? Of course he is a loving Father, but he is still our Lord too, and as such there must be times when he has to say, 'That is something I cannot give you or tell you, nor can I even tell you why. Trust me.'

Chapter 11

Prayer for healing

Before we can understand when, how, and possibly whether, to pray for healing, we need to examine sickness in all its forms, and know something of how healing processes work.

Physical sickness can be any malfunction of the body. It can be caused by an accident, germ, virus, failure or wearing out of any part of the body or, as with cancer, a self-destructive cause we don't yet fully understand.

Mental sickness is the inability of the mind to function properly, so that rational and creative thought, memory and self-esteem are impaired. The cause can be a complex mixture of social and cultural influences, suffering, fear, indoctrination, abuse and persecution, and may be rooted in upbringing or other experiences long past.

Another type of sickness, of which we understand even less, is spiritual sickness. This could mean being under the control of supernatural forces, possibly as a result of getting involved with occult practices or influences, or it could be ill-health resulting from a deep-seated sense of guilt or other cause. In the New Testament, it is described as being possessed by a demon or evil spirit, an expression that was also used to cover mental illness or epilepsy, which is not surprising when we consider that in the time of Jesus they understood little about anatomy and knew nothing at all about bacteria, let alone viruses.

For the same reason, it is not surprising that they assumed all sickness, other than that caused by accidents, to be God-sent retribution for sin. If a man was mugged on the barren Jerusalem–Jericho road, the robber was obviously at fault, but if someone was suddenly struck down with acute stomach pains, skin disease or paralysis, another explanation had to be found. The most likely one seemed to them to be that God was punishing him for something.

In most illnesses, physical disorders give rise to symptoms (pain, swelling, loss of appetite, *etc.*) and it is mainly by these symptoms the illness is diagnosed. The situation is complicated by the fact that it is possible to have the symptoms without the physical disorders. That is, there can be a mental problem that is manifesting itself in physical symptoms. The situation is still further complicated by the fact that physical disorders can cause mental problems, which may themselves be a manifestation of *spiritual* malaise.

It is only comparatively recently that the complex interrelationships between body, mind and spirit have been considered. We are still a long way from giving them the attention they deserve. Why is it that we sometimes hear of the miraculous disappearance of backaches but not of boils? Or of cancer, but not of varicose veins? It clearly has something to do with symptoms we can see and those we can't, but there's more to it than that. We have a lot more to learn about the way God works in our minds and bodies.

Physical illness caused by emotional problems is called 'psychosomatic', and calls for teamwork between medical and psychiatric doctors and religious counsellors. Unfortunately, this 'total' treatment of a patient, which we call 'holistic medicine', is still all too rare.

Henry, in our typical prayer meeting, is a good example. He recently lost his wife and has to go through the bereavement process. He is not finding it easy to make the adjustment from being one of a working partnership to being self-sufficient. This is never easy, but most people manage it by a combination of courage and common-sense – and, if they are Christians, the assurance that, because of God's love and the redeeming work of Jesus, death is not final. This, with the comfort and help of family and friends, sees them through.

But Henry could not accept his loss. Perhaps part of the reason is that women usually live longer than men, so that he was unprepared for widowerhood; and sometimes men are less capable of coping with the practicalities of living alone than women. Anyway, Henry resented being alone; he never actually said so, and perhaps wasn't even aware of it, but to him, life was unfair.

Before long, he began to be unwell. He had back pains, and couldn't go out. The doctor prescribed rest and arranged an X-ray. That failed to indicate the cause, so he prescribed painkilling drugs. The pain was relieved, but other symptoms appeared. So did other drugs. Because he was 'ill' and not just sorry for himself, he received visits and sympathy. They provided therapy that the drugs, not surprisingly, had failed to provide. But not for long. Compassion fatigue set in, and visits dwindled.

The doctor failed because he treated the symptoms and not the cause. No psychiatrist was involved, because physical symptoms are taken to indicate physical problems. A minister couldn't help, except by showing concern and compassion, because Henry didn't really believe that God could do what doctors couldn't. The friends stopped helping because they didn't understand. They said, 'It's all in the mind', as though that made the symptoms harmless, whereas the symptoms were real enough and the pain was genuine. The combined efforts of doctors, nurses, radiologist, dietician, physiotherapist, a minister, family and friends, not to mention many expensive drugs, failed to bring healing.

This inability to discover the root cause of ill-health is very common. Depression, for example, can have its roots in guilt or fear, with the result that patients may receive drugs when what they really need is forgiveness or the knowledge of God's powerful care.

We therefore see that before any healing can take place, the cause of the sickness must be discovered. This may be obvious, but sometimes the cause is so deep in the subconscious or so far in the past that it is very difficult to trace. Praying for healing may involve asking for wisdom to discern the underlying reasons for the sickness. In Henry's case, there is the danger of praying for relief from pain or debility, when the prayer should be that he be 'made whole', to use a term that Jesus used.

If we ignore the cause and just consider the symptoms, there is a danger that the sickness will not be cured, or, if it is, that it will recur. This in fact is what many doctors do. No-one can blame them; they have so many patients to deal with that they have no time for lengthy consultations and may be able to do no more than make superficial diagnoses and write a prescription. I know of one doctor who declared that he never cured anybody; he just alleviated their symptoms to give their illnesses a chance to heal themselves.

It may be a reaction to this policy of just prescribing drugs to combat symptoms, or it may be the increase of side-effects (drugs easing one symptom but creating another), that has given rise to the wider use of new techniques that we call 'alternative medicine'. Actually, they are not all new. Acupuncture, for example (inserting and rotating needles at strategic points), originated in ancient China, although it was not until the 1970s that it began to be used in the West. It is now, like chiropractic (spinal manipulation) and homeopathy (energizing the body's own healing processes), slowly becoming accepted in the medical world. Other techniques, such as aromatherapy and massage, are not generally regarded by the medical profession as curative, although they may well instil a feeling of well-being, which in turn makes the patient feel healthier.

The more we consider the relationship between feeling well and being well, the more we realize we are in a very grey area indeed. It is now accepted that smoking is regarded as creating a feel-good factor at the expense of damaging our bodies. It is buying short-term pleasure or comfort at the expense of future ill-health. But then so are overeating, heavy drinking, drug taking (and that may even include some tranquillizers prescribed by your doctor), avoiding fresh air and never walking when you can ride.

Having looked at the things that cause illness, or that prevent the wholeness that God intends for us, we can look at how God heals. Most people divide healing into human (based on the medical and pharmaceutical professions) and spiritual (based on miracles wrought by faith). I suggest that this is an oversimplification. There are *three* ways in which God heals, and they are closely connected.

The first is indeed through medicine – doctors, nurses, drugs and so on. It is nonsense to say that spiritual healing is God's province while the medical profession is a human activity. There would be no medical profession without God. It is God who has revealed all the knowledge they use and given all the skill they apply.

Every day, many thousands of people are being made well, whether in hospitals, clinics or at home, by treatment, by drugs, and by tender loving care. Many of the doctors, surgeons and nurses will have chosen their vocation as part of their Christian commitment, as will many physiotherapists, porters and all the others who play a part in restoring health. God works through skilled and dedicated people, through drugs, and through hi-tech equipment, to give healing and wholeness.

The second is by the activity of the Holy Spirit in the mind and body of the patient, effecting a cure in answer to the prayers of that person or of someone else at his or her request. This may be called divine healing, faith healing or miraculous healing, but those descriptions can be misleading, as we shall see; spiritual healing is a better term.

The third way – and the one some people fail to notice – is by the continual process of repair and renewal that goes on in our bodies all the time. We all know that the cells that make up our bodies are constantly being renewed, and God uses this as a healing process. It doesn't depend on prayer, or on faith – it just happens. It is a part of God's continuous creativity.

If you cut a finger, it will get better without prayer or professional treatment. You will speed the process by cleaning the cut and covering it with a plaster or bandage to prevent infection (thus co-operating with God by providing the conditions that best help natural healing), but the cut will normally heal anyway. The same is true of many other ailments and malfunctions, both of body and of mind. Colds disappear, backs stop aching and depression gives way to cheerfulness again without anybody asking for it or taking any medical action. God's healing is in us all the time. We should remember that fact when people talk about divine healing.

We should be grateful that these three ways of

healing exist. All three have their place. It would be nonsense to say that we don't need spiritual healing now that we have antibiotics, just as it would be nonsense to say that we don't need doctors or nurses if we have faith.

So what does all this have to say about our praying for healing? We base our prayers on two convictions. The first is that *all* healing originates with God. We can co-operate with him through medicines, nursing and prayer, but of ourselves we cannot heal anyone. The second is that God wants all his creatures to enjoy good health. That does not mean that if we are Christians, health is something to which we have an inalienable right, because there may be good reasons why God allows us to suffer.

As we saw earlier, sickness is sometimes the result of our own folly. We may become ill by treating our bodies unwisely – for instance, eating too much and exercising too little. The cure, if it is not too late, is in our own hands. Or we may refuse to do something God has asked us to do. That may rob us of peace of mind, and that in turn may cause depression or even manifest itself in physical symptoms. The cure requires self-examination, repentance and obedience.

The apostle Paul wrote about being 'controlled by the Spirit', and he was well aware that our human nature all too often resumes control. We therefore stand in constant need of re-submitting our lives to the Holy Spirit's direction. That is one way of keeping in line with God's plans for us, which obviously include a healthy lifestyle and therefore, probably but not inevitably, good health. This is something we also pray for others, but it did not figure in our typical prayer meeting.

It remains true that there is much suffering and ill-health that is not in any way self-inflicted. How can we reconcile that with the statement that God wants us to be well? The Bible, and our own experience, teach us that God sometimes allows us to suffer bodily or mentally in order that his purposes may be carried out, which ultimately turns out for our higher good.

Remember Paul and his 'thorn in the flesh'? That is only one of many biblical examples of the necessity of being willing to suffer for the sake of the gospel. The most obvious one is that of our Saviour himself. He endured the ultimate in suffering (no, not the crucifixion in itself, but taking our sins on himself); the result was the ultimate in triumph.

We all know that suffering is a necessary part of life – this life, that is. Or perhaps you don't. If so, try to imagine a completely suffering-free world – one in which *everything* that happened was enjoyable. You would soon realize that happiness depends on the possibility of losing it. An old song declared that 'into each life some rain must fall'. Notice the 'must'. We could no more go through life without suffering than we could have light without darkness; each depends on an awareness of the other.

Although we can learn through suffering, have our characters refined by it, or see God glorified in it, very often the reason for it will still baffle us. Ill-health is only one aspect of suffering, but it is an area where God in his wisdom may have to say no to our requests for healing. Prayer is an expression of our natural concern, a request to understand the cause, and a plea for wholeness by whichever means God chooses to use, always on the understanding that in his wisdom he may have a purpose in allowing the illness to continue.

Prayer should not be seen as instant therapy. It sometimes happens that people who have heard of dramatic healings will pray for healing – for themselves or others – and then, because no improvement is seen the next morning, will conclude that God has not healed them; when in fact he *is doing* just that.

We have already seen that the cure may be in the patient's own hands. In that case, if you are the patient, God's answer must be, 'Do it yourself.' If you are praying for someone else who is – in part, at least – damaging his or her own health, perhaps by an unhealthy diet or lifestyle, you may need to say to that person, 'You can effect, or at least materially assist in, your own cure.' That may require a great deal of courage and graciousness, but it is real Christian fellowship in action.

There are many other cases where praying for our own healing will be very different from praying for someone else's. For myself I may say, 'I will not pray for healing. If God wants me to get better, it will happen, and if he doesn't, he will help me to accept the situation.' That can be difficult, but it does help me to accept God's will, reminds me that he has me in his hands, and keeps open the possibility of God pointing me towards a hidden cause or need to be dealt with.

If it were someone else who needed healing, however, it would not be right to refuse to pray for him or her on that basis.

Recalling our typical prayer meeting again, what do we pray for Mrs Hodges? First, that God by his Spirit will give comfort of body, peace of mind and freedom from fear. Secondly, that the healing process will be successful and not protracted. Thirdly, for all the medical staff involved, thanking God for their skill and dedication. All this must be combined with a determination to take practical steps to share in the healing process, by visiting with some flowers, talc, tissues or something to read, or whatever else needs to be done.

In the case of Jean's colleague's uncle, one thing to do is to ask Jean to find out more about the situation as soon as she can. In the meantime, it is right to ask for the strengthening and peace-giving power of the Holy Spirit for Jean's colleague as well as for her uncle; and to ask Jean to tell her colleague that they are praying.

Mary raises special considerations. What you do depends on what you know of her. If you know she is something of a hypochondriac, then your prayer should concentrate on asking God to give her full assurance of his protection. On no account dismiss her plea as merely neurotic; whatever the cause and however wrong her dramatic diagnosis may be, her need is real.

However, it may be that Mary is absolutely right – her work for her Master really *is* attracting Satan's attention, in which case your prayers for the Spirit's overshadowing will be important. They should concentrate on claiming scriptural promises, not expressing hopes.

We now have to face the question of how we know when to go to the doctor, when to ask God for healing, and when to do nothing, trusting God to make us well or help us to accept the situation; or, if it is someone else who is ill, what to advise the sufferer to do. Do we ask for healing, claim it, hope for it or follow prescribed treatment?

It depends on the sickness. For example, if you had dandruff, would you pray for it to clear up or change your shampoo? If you had a headache, would you fall on your knees or reach for the paracetamol? Moving up to something that is still comparatively trivial but might be regarded as terribly serious by a teenager, would you pray to be rid of acne? Extending this: for relief from arthritis? Or to be healed of a brain tumour?

The point of these questions is not that I want to know the answers (even if you could tell me), but to get you to think about *why* or *when* you ask for healing. Let's take the questions further. What would you pray for, if anything, if you were diabetic? Or if you lost a leg in a car accident? Or if you'd been profoundly deaf from birth? Or if you were HIV positive?

It must be true that God can, if he chooses, deal with any problem from a wasp sting to a cataract to terminal cancer, from being 'down in the dumps' to drug dependency to schizophrenia. Experience tells us that some of these (and not only the missing leg!) are less likely to respond to prayer for healing than others. Why?

The reason lies partly in the nature of spiritual healing, and partly in the mental and spiritual state of the patient and whoever is asked to pray for healing. Some people have a low pain threshold while others can take acute pain in their stride. Some people complain at the slightest discomfort while others accept illness and suffering stoically. Some people have confidence that God can and will make them well while others have great difficulty in believing it. All these have a bearing on the efficacy of prayer for healing.

As we look at the way spiritual healing operates, the part played by faith, and the importance of praying in the name of Jesus, we can begin to answer some of the questions we have posed. But don't expect them all to be answered, because there is, and always will be in this life, an element of mystery in how, when and why God releases his healing power.

There are five basic rules that we *can* be sure of. These are for when you are the sick person:

1. Do what you can for yourself by having a healthy lifestyle.

2. Use whatever medical facilities are available; they too are God-given.

3. Never doubt that God *can* heal, but never demand that he *must*. He knows best.

4. Be sure that God hears and responds. If he appears not to, ask why, always on the understanding that he may have good reason for not telling you why.

5. Remember that you are mortal.

If you are thinking of others who are ill, you will encourage them, where appropriate, to follow those five rules. You will also have a place for them in your prayers and give time to help in practical ways if you can.

Chapter 12

Miracles and faith

For some people, praying for healing means praying for a miracle. They lay hands on the patient and specifically ask God to remove the pain or illness immediately and dramatically. What's more, God sometimes does it.

At other times, he doesn't. Where patients have been led to believe that their healing is directly related to their faith, this may do more damage to their faith than the illness is doing to their bodies.

But what exactly is a miracle and what is its purpose?

Take a simple example. Betty arrives just in time for the prayer meeting, her face beaming. Just as she was leaving home, the phone rang (doesn't it always?). As a result she left late and was sure she would miss her bus and have to wait ages for the next one. As she hurried along the road, she prayed that a bus would come soon, and just as she got to the bus stop, it came along.

Was that a miracle or a coincidence? We'll answer that a bit later on.

Another example. Betty is on her way to the bus stop when she realizes she has left her purse at home. If she goes home for it, she'll miss the bus for sure. She prays. Then a few paces away, she spots a 50p piece on the ground – just enough for her fare. Miracle or coincidence? Both. The coin was obviously there before she prayed; God didn't quickly put it there and then make sure she spotted it. To that extent it was a coincidence. But the fact still remains that she needed her bus fare, prayed, and immediately received it. If that's not a miracle, what is?

From a tiny miracle to a big one. We've already referred to Elijah on Mount Carmel, asking God to send fire from heaven. We could easily dismiss that as a coincidence. It was probably a stroke of lightning – a storm is not unusual at the end of a period of drought. They were on high ground and the altar was soaked with water – just the place where lightning would strike. So we've explained the miracle away, haven't we?

Have we? For lightning to strike *that* spot at *that* moment, just as Elijah had finished praying – of course it was a miracle!

One more example from the Bible. Imagine Abraham on Mount Moriah about to offer his son Isaac as a sacrifice as God had instructed him. They have come three days' journey from their home. The altar is built, and Isaac, bound, is laid on it. Abraham raises his knife ready to plunge it into the boy's heart when he hears a voice. He is told that Isaac is not to be harmed; it was a test of obedience and he had passed.

But a sacrifice is still needed. Abraham looks round and sees a ram caught in a bush by its horns. A coincidence – it just *happened* to be there? It is unusual for animals to get caught like that in their natural habitat – but *that* ram was in *that* bush at the exact moment when Abraham needed him. Of course it was a miracle! So Abraham was quite right when he declared that God had provided. (Incidentally, he was foreshadowing the time when God would provide another, and much greater, sacrifice – Jesus – at that same place.)

Back to Betty and the bus that arrived 'to order'. We must ask ourselves what would have happened if Betty hadn't prayed. The bus would have come anyway because it must have been on its way before Betty prayed. It was not at its scheduled time, but it must have been on its way although not yet in sight; it didn't just materialize. So surely Betty's prayer had nothing to do with it.

Don't be so sure. You see, God *knew* that Betty would be late that day and he knew she would pray. Of course he did; his infinite knowledge means that he knows everything that has ever happened and that ever will happen.

Is it actually possible that the Lord of heaven and earth should make provision to meet a trivial request from an ordinary person who wants to catch a bus? It's a staggering thought, but I believe the answer is, 'Yes, it is.' What a truly wonderful God and Father he is!

This raises a question that has bothered Christians

for centuries: the conflict between free will and predestination. The argument runs like this. If God knows all about everything, he must know everything that is ever *going* to happen. So whatever he foresees *will* happen. Therefore, what is the point of – well, praying, for one thing? If God already knows what we are going to ask for and whether we are going to get it, why ask? It's a waste of time.

Equally, we could say (and people have) that there is no point in evangelism, since God has already decided who will commit their lives to him and who won't. The way to approach this 'problem' is to look first at free will. The Bible tells us that when God made human beings, he made them 'like himself'. We are well aware that there are many ways in which we are nothing like God at all, but the similarity is that we were given the ability to know right from wrong, and the responsibility to choose between them. This is what distinguishes us from animals. They follow instincts; we make moral choices.

Every day of our lives, we use this power to choose, in matters large and small, from what cereal to have for breakfast to who we want to marry. For example, I remember many years ago deciding to follow Jesus. I thought it through, and I decided. I wasn't a puppet, I wasn't programmed. It was my choice. It is true that the Holy Spirit had a hand in that decision, but I was the one who chose, and no-one can deny me the benefit of that experience.

Now let's turn our attention to God. We believe there is absolutely nothing he does not know or cannot do. He is not limited in any way at all. So yes, he does know everything that will ever happen, including every decision any of us will ever make.

We therefore have to accept that *both* statements are true – that we choose and that God knows. We cannot *understand* how both can be true. That remains a mystery, like many other aspects of the spiritual realm that our earthbound minds are unable to take in. We can't understand space going on for ever and ever, but then we can't imagine it stopping either. If it does, what lies beyond the point where it stops? No, infinity remains a mystery to our human minds, as does eternity.

This inability to accept that our decisions are not invalid just because God knew about them beforehand has been the cause of great discord and division in the church for many centuries. There are still many Christians today who are firmly for *either* free will or predestination. To them, it is a simple matter of logic. But in matters of faith, we are in the spiritual realm where earthly logic is left behind.

We must therefore make our decisions (and persuade others to make choices too, which is what evangelism involves) while never doubting that God has the whole universe under his eternal control. So, however hard it is to comprehend God's infinite knowledge, be sure that when we pray, he hears and responds – or perhaps 'has responded'.

Now we can answer the question we began with: what is a miracle, and what is its purpose? A miracle is any striking event that defies, or appears to defy, natural law, thereby demonstrating God's control over creation and his ability to achieve whatever he desires.

Notice that it can be any event, big or small, and it makes no difference whether you can see a logical explanation for the event or it leaves you baffled.

In the case of healing, if there is any attempt or desire by the sick person, or by someone who is praying for that person, to claim any credit, the healing is unlikely to happen. That is why Jesus consistently refused to work miracles to satisfy the curious and the sceptics. He was not prepared to use God's power to justify himself to faithless critics any more than he was prepared to use it to save himself from the cross.

The purpose of a miracle is therefore to demonstrate God's power and bring glory to him. It is given to encourage us and strengthen our faith, and *never* just for our satisfaction. If Betty thought she could start getting buses whenever she liked, she'd have to think again. We have already seen that prayer doesn't work like that.

Perhaps that is why these 'mundane miracles' are usually experienced by new Christians. As faith matures, the need for these small but exciting proofs of God's greatness gives way to a steady trust. Until that happens, we should never dismiss them. New faith needs the humus of encouragement in the soil of good teaching if it is to grow.

Indeed, miracles in the Bible are often referred to as 'signs', and that is exactly what they are. Whether they are small and personal, or striking enough to make headline news, they are signs of both the power and the love of God.

It's just as well that the exercise of God's healing power cannot be controlled by our faith or our actions, because if it were, what an awful responsibility would be laid on us! Imagine it. Someone is ill; I pray; healing comes. If that happened because I prayed, I am then at the mercy of anyone else who is ill because I obviously cannot refuse to help anyone in need.

Fortunately, the healing power, and the decision to use it, are both in God's hands, and there they stay. There are no such people as 'miracle workers' who have acquired the power to heal, although it is true that God does choose some people more than others *through* whom to exercise a healing ministry. Jesus went about Galilee bringing healing to many people, but there were many more that he didn't heal. That's not because there were those he could not heal, or didn't want to, but because God alone chooses how and when his almighty power operates.

Faith

What part does faith play in prayer for healing, whether for ourselves or others? It is vital, in three ways. We should believe in God's power (he is able to do as we ask); in his love (he always wants the best for us); and in his wisdom (he may have good reasons for *not* doing as we ask). That does not mean that God insists on our reaching a certain level of faith before he will act. God heals primarily because he loves us and wants us to be well. He heals atheists as well as Christians.

Let's go back to our definition of prayer – laying our thoughts before God and letting him change them as he will. There is obviously no point in doing that if we do not believe with all our hearts that God can and will change us and that that change will be for our good.

If we have no faith in God, we cut ourselves off from this process; we disconnect ourselves from the spiritual power circuit. So faith in God (in his perfect love as well as his almighty power) is the basis on which we put our lives completely under his control. It therefore governs all our praying and not just prayers for healing.

That raises the question of how we acquire faith in the first place. Fortunately, it is a gift of the Holy Spirit and one that he is always ready to bestow if we ask him in humility and sincerity. In fact, God is more ready to give us faith than we are to ask for it, because of our earthbound natures. That means that praying for faith may be a necessary prelude to many of our other prayers, both in private and when praying with others.

Let us look at the part played by faith in the healing of the lame man by the apostle Peter. When we study the passage (in Acts 3) we notice that the healing is all of a piece with the message Peter gave in the temple just afterwards. It was as though the healing was a God-given visual aid.

Notice four things. First, there is no question of a spurious healing, one in which a person has an imaginary or self-induced ailment which disappears when he is prayed for. The writer, Luke (a doctor, remember), points out that his 'feet and ankles became strong'. Something physical happened.

Secondly, it was God's power that effected the healing. It is made very clear that Peter acted only as a channel, while the lame man did nothing at all.

Thirdly, notice the use of the vital phrase 'in the

name of Jesus Christ of Nazareth' at the healing, and 'in his name' in the subsequent explanation. Peter was complying with the instructions Jesus gave in the discourse recorded in John 14 – 16.

Finally, look at the use of the words 'by faith' and 'it was faith in Jesus that has made him well'. The healing power was God's; the 'password' that invoked it was 'by faith in the name of Jesus'. Those words contain three vital elements. One, a recognition that Jesus, and no-one else, was the revealer of God. Two, a submission to God's will. Three, a total belief that God's power could achieve the desired result. There are times when submission to God may mean accepting that healing will not be given, but in this case Peter was clearly confident it would, and that was because the Holy Spirit had given him the necessary faith.

We see similar principles at work in the letter of James, chapter 5. He advises sick people to send for the church elders, who will pray for them and rub oil on them 'in the name of the Lord. This prayer made in faith will heal the sick.'

The use of olive oil in this case is for remedial purposes and should not be confused with being anointed for a great task as when a prophet anointed a king. Nor should it be deduced that oil has any magic properties. This is significant because it suggests that we should not abandon whatever medical remedies are available to us. Prayer for healing should be used with them, not instead of them.

In this passage, healing is closely connected with forgiveness. We know that Jesus expressly denied the prevailing Jewish notion that sickness was a punishment for sin, but that is not to deny the close link between forgiveness and health.

In fact, this link gives us one clue as to how spiritual healing often works. We all know that guilt destroys any feeling of well-being, although we may not realize the extent of it because guilt is so often suppressed. We also know that one of the worst aspects of sickness is fear, whether of pain, increasing inability to cope or to achieve, or the possibility of permanent disability or death.

Most of us can stand more pain than we think we can, once we accept it instead of regarding it as something that is wrong. Most of us can adjust to disability when we have to. Most of us can face death bravely after we have come to terms with its inevitability. But we are afraid of these things because we think they simply shouldn't happen – at least, not to us.

Now suppose we could eliminate both guilt and fear. The resulting experience of calm content, and the deep joy of being cleansed (by being forgiven) and unafraid (because we know the Holy Spirit is with us), would give full rein to God's continual process of renewal. The result is healing – wholeness of body and mind.

None of us would expect spiritual healing to be effective in replacing a missing limb or carrying out a transplant. But what about somebody deformed from birth or who has been disabled for years; or is suffering from dementia or Alzheimer's disease in old age? We should never doubt God's power to heal if he chooses to do so, whatever the problem – diseased organs, defective limbs, tortured minds, anything. He who created can re-create. That means that there may be many situations when we decide not to ask for healing; we just ask God to help us humbly accept that his perfect wisdom is beyond our understanding. This applies particularly to prayer for ourselves but it also applies to our praying for others.

Spiritual healing, then, is not so much a case of spiritual forces working directly on our physical bodies, as of God's power setting our minds and hearts completely at rest, thus allowing physical healing to take place, sometimes instantaneously, sometimes over a period of time. This highlights the importance of living in such a way that, as far as possible, we always have a clear conscience and a constant trust in God as our loving Father. With our minds and hearts thus at ease, we are more likely to experience the wholeness God wants for us, instead of a series of healings between bouts of illness or depression. There is no better advertisement for spiritual healing than not to need it.

There are two more biblical passages we should look at when we are considering the place of faith in healing. One is Acts 5:15, where we are told that 'sick people were carried out into the streets and placed on beds and mats so that at least Peter's shadow might fall on some of them as he passed by'. The other is Acts 19:12, where we read: 'Even handkerchiefs and aprons he [Paul] had used were taken to those who were ill and their diseases were driven away'.

At first sight, this is sheer superstition. But it worked. We must therefore conclude that if sick people have faith in God (that is, believe he has the power, and the will, to make them whole), and if they recognize that it is only because Jesus has made God's true nature known to us that we can ask for that power to be used, it doesn't matter what words or articles are used, or how great or how little is the involvement of the person through whom the request is made.

In theory, presumably there need not be another person involved at all, but in practice it would seem to be necessary. We can see the reason for this by recalling that the Holy Spirit's power must always be used for God's glory, not ours. The involvement of more than one person means that faith and submission must be openly declared as a prelude to the prayer for healing. Similarly, the use of something that *cannot* have any remedial properties, like a shadow or a handkerchief, makes it clear that a supernatural power is at work.

To sum up. Prayers for healing, like other prayers, should not tell God what to do, and still less how and when to do it. An important part of our Christian lives is to bring our concerns for health and wholeness to our Father for ourselves (a great privilege) and for others (still a privilege but also a duty). For our own health, the more we trust God to look after us, and the more we thank him for the health we do enjoy, the better. For other people, we should be ready to give plenty of time to pray and even more to act out our concern with practical help.

Chapter 13

The first lesson on prayer

(This chapter is based on Matthew 6:5–15 and Luke 11:1–4.)

It is right to regard the Lord's Prayer very highly; it is quite wrong to assume it teaches us all we need to know about prayer. We must not forget it was given by Jesus to his disciples as Lesson 1.

The disciples had no doubt been watching Jesus at prayer. They knew too that he sometimes went off to pray all night by himself. They knew the strength he derived from it. It is not surprising they wanted to know the secret. So they made a simple request to their Master: 'Lord, teach us to pray, just as John taught his disciples.' In reply, Jesus gave them a simple (but very profound) example to follow.

One thing we can be sure of is that Jesus' teaching on prayer was not a bit like that of his cousin, John the Baptist. John would have taught his disciples to be humble, to be repentant, and above all, to be reverent.

His prayers would have followed the pattern of the Psalms with which all Jews were familiar, emphasizing God's law and the need to obey it. Jesus began by saying, 'Father.'

The need for humility and reverence are still there, but the invocation of a remote and all-powerful God was replaced by a family conversation. That must have been difficult for the disciples to grasp, and we modern disciples still find it hard to rejoice in talking to God as our Father while still retaining a sense of awe in his presence. Thinking about God as the Creator and Lord of all, but also as our loving Father, is an essential prelude to the rest of the prayer. It is like tuning in. It may take time before we feel we've really made contact.

We need not worry. Simply because he *is* our Father, he understands the difficulty, and we talk to him as naturally as children always talk to their fathers, so long as we do not allow familiarity to breed disrespect.

The Lord's Prayer begins with worship. The disciples – that's us, now – were to exalt the name of God, to give him honour, to acknowledge his almighty power and perfect wisdom. Putting God before and above all else was the hallmark of Jewish worship and should be the hallmark of ours.

Then comes the first request – that God's kingdom should be established on earth, that his rule should hold sway on earth as it does in his presence in glory. That is an easy request to make until we remember what it involves. For one thing, this request takes precedence over anything we want to ask for ourselves. Then, it implies that we must accept God's total rule over *our* lives before we can expect it to apply to others. Finally, it must remind us that we have a part to play in the establishment of that kingdom. There's a whole agenda in that sentence.

Now we make a request for ourselves – for our daily food. But in view of all the other things Jesus taught about trusting God to provide for our needs, this is more of a reminder to ourselves that God will care for us than a request that he will. We have only to read the passage in the Sermon on the Mount about God feeding the birds and clothing the wild flowers to realize that. He was constantly teaching people that they should give up fretting and start trusting.

It may seem strange in a book on prayer to be told that many Christians pray when they shouldn't. But they do. They keep on asking when they should be trusting. In the Sermon on the Mount, Jesus reminded the crowds that they need not worry about the necessities of life, like food and clothes, because 'your Father in heaven knows that you need all these things'.

But many Christians find it hard really to believe that if we put our lives into God's hands, he accepts responsibility for caring for us. We do not find trusting easy, because our instincts are to look after our needs; but we must never allow trust to become the forgotten factor in our Christian lives. It is a good test of spiritual maturity.

It is therefore not surprising that there is no prayer for our wants, only for our needs. God in his great love and goodness gives us so many things to enjoy, but they *are* gifts, not entitlements. There should be no place in our prayers for selfish demands, even if we see people around us with much more than we have.

We ourselves may not need to pray for our 'daily bread', but there are those who do, so it is worth sparing a thought for those who may face a new day without knowing what, or whether, they will eat that day. This may involve us in praying for the aid agencies that try to support them, or better still, resolving to support one of those agencies.

Next, we ask for forgiveness. This bothers some people. 'Surely,' they say, 'the forgiveness we received when we committed our lives to Jesus was complete. Why then do we need to be forgiven again?' We will look at the impact of salvation on our lives in a moment, but for now let's say that we need forgiveness because we are still sinners. Aren't we? We are all too aware that we constantly fail to live up to the standards that following Jesus calls for.

It was something the apostle Paul described very vividly in one of his letters, where he wrote, 'I don't do what I would like to do, but instead I do what I hate.' We know the feeling. The effect of any sin sets up a barrier between ourselves and the person hurt; and also between us and God. (That word 'sin', by the way, is one that we often use too carelessly. It becomes more real if we think of it as anything mean, selfish, cruel, dishonest or unworthy. Or lazy, insensitive or uncaring, since *not* doing something can be a sin too.)

Forgiveness is love in action, getting rid of that barrier, repairing the relationship, and re-creating harmony. This simple request in the Lord's Prayer is therefore difficult, because we have to let his light shine on things we'd prefer to hide; and vitally important, because we cannot live fully under the control of the Holy Spirit until this restoring process has taken place.

Before we go on, let us examine that question of the forgiveness we receive when we commit our lives to Jesus as Saviour. Yes, it is complete – in the sense that it is not partial. Everything we have ever done wrong, from unkind thoughts to vile crime, is blotted out. At that moment we begin a new *spiritual* life, and that life, like all new lives, is completely innocent, untainted by any stain of sin. We don't look any different, and, surprisingly, may not feel any different, but we are. Because Jesus took our sins on himself on the cross, and because we committed our lives into his keeping, God *counts us* as righteous. If you like long words, it is called the doctrine of justification, or being 'put right with God'. Paul had a good deal to say about it, but somehow this wonderful truth was largely overlooked for centuries. Eventually, Martin Luther and others rediscovered it, and the Reformation was born.

Unfortunately, being justified does not mean becoming perfect, as we all know only too well. Our old natures do not just disappear; we soon find ourselves saying and doing things that Christians shouldn't. It *is* God's clear intention that we should become perfect, but that is a slow process, and will take more than the rest of our lives. That is called (here's another long word) sanctification – being made holy.

As nothing unclean or unworthy can exist in God's eternal kingdom (and that is our destination), when this life is over we will finally become the creatures God has always intended us to be. Until then, we can be –

indeed, will be – unkind, selfish, and all the other things we know we shouldn't be. So we need to confess, repent, and be forgiven. Repentance, by the way, is more than confession. Confession is simply owning up to doing wrong. Even that can be hard enough, but repentance is a very different thing; it includes regretting the wrong, promising to make restitution where possible, and determining never to do it again. There's not a lot of that about.

Getting back to the Lord's Prayer, if asking for forgiveness can be difficult, the next part of the prayer can be shattering! Jesus flatly declared that our being forgiven was dependent on our being willing to forgive anyone who has, or we think has, wronged us. The forgiveness that is so important to us will be denied us all the time we go on bearing a grudge or a feeling of resentment or bitterness towards anyone else. There must be times when, if we are honest, there will be a long gap in our praying at this point.

If we have an unforgiving attitude towards a particular person or group, it poisons our relationship with them and also with God, so we will have to wrestle with it. Fortunately, the same Holy Spirit who effects our forgiveness is ready to help us forgive others. He is always working at reconciliation, healing, restoring, creating understanding and putting love in place of hate.

The prayer then moves on to a plea that God will direct us away from what is sinful and therefore harmful, and protect us from Satan's attacks. This could be, but shouldn't be, interpreted as supporting separatism, the idea of keeping clear of all contact with unbelievers. It *can't* mean that, because it was not long after teaching his disciples this prayer that Jesus sent them out on an evangelistic mission.

There is no way in which Christians can keep themselves to themselves in a world in which we are called to be light (to show the truth), salt (to preserve from decay) and leaven (to influence for good). We are already too prone to stay in barracks when we should be on the battlefield; or to enjoy fellowship with each other when we should be making the gospel known to others; or to look after ourselves when we should be involved in compassionate service to a needy world.

What this prayer *does* ask is that God will keep us in the way he has chosen for us; that he will guide us day by day, helping us to avoid everything that would draw us away from him, dishonour his name, or detract from the quality of our service. That guidance is sure to involve us in situations in which Satan will try to intervene, so the prayer goes on to ask that when that happens, the Holy Spirit will be our shield as well as our sword.

That was the end of the prayer as Jesus taught it to his disciples, but we always add a sentence that reaffirms our awareness of God's sovereignty, power and majesty. So we should. It is good to end our prayer, as we began it, in worship.

One very obvious omission from the Lord's Prayer is the very thing that our prayer meetings largely consist of, and that is prayer for others: 'intercession' is the word we use for it. It cannot be because Jesus thought it unnecessary; we know that just before his arrest he prayed for Peter 'that your faith will not fail'. Then in John's gospel we have what we call his high-priestly prayer, in which he prayed for his disciples in every generation; he actually had you and me in mind even in his hour of greatest suffering.

Right at the beginning of most of the apostle Paul's letters, there is a reference to the fact that he prays for his readers constantly. In the letter to Rome, for example, he writes, 'God knows that I remember you every time I pray' – and at that time he hadn't even been to Rome. In one of his letters to Corinth, after a long list of his sufferings as an apostle, he goes on, '... not to mention other things, every day I am under the pressure of my concern for all the churches'. There is certainly no doubt about the need for intercessory prayer.

You have probably discovered that it is all too easy to promise to pray for people and then forget to do it. Such a promise should not be made lightly, and, if it is made, it is important to honour it. It may be possible to pray with them there and then, or immediately after leaving them (or coming off the phone). If not, make a written note somewhere, say on a calendar or in a diary.

Why, then, did Jesus not include any requests on behalf of others in the prayer he taught his disciples? The first reason is that the things he did include are the sort of things that are always relevant, whereas prayer for current needs and situations is, in the nature of things, always changing. That does not mean that every time we pray we must include everything that is in the Lord's Prayer, but that those things must never be lost sight of. They are fundamental, providing a basic framework for our prayers.

The second reason is that praying for others, if it is to be effective, calls for the sort of thoughtful understanding of what we are doing that only comes with experience; after all, I did say the Lord's Prayer was Lesson 1! That is, we often need to spend time asking God what to ask him for before we ask it. That is the part we too often omit. We treat God as a fairy godmother instead of a wise Father. The fact that he knows what we need before we ask it is no excuse; part of the reason we pray is that we should bring our wills into line with his, and then make our requests on the basis of what he shows us.

If there is one thing more than any other that will rob the Lord's Prayer of its value, it is dropping into the way of reciting it unthinkingly. Much as we treasure the familiar words, what matters is to keep the meaning fresh. This can be done in several ways.

The Anglican *Alternative Service Book* has a version in which the language has been updated, and there is no reason why others should not be written by whoever is leading worship, being included on a service sheet or displayed on an overhead projector. If preferred, a version could be written in the form of a psalm, in which the congregation make their responses.

In some churches, the Lord's Prayer is sung rather than spoken, but if this is always the same words to the same tune, the problem of over-familiarity remains. In my own church, we occasionally use a rhymed paraphrase sung to the tune of 'Annie's Song' (the words are given in Appendix 2). Another possibility is to use it as a pattern or outline, with each section acting as a heading or prompt for extempore, open, or silent prayer.

Let us then learn from the Lord's Prayer and use it to guide our meditations, but be sure that God has yet much more to teach us about prayer. We will learn it only as we go on praying. In fact, we could describe prayer as a continuing process of learning about God.

Chapter 14

God didn't answer

Oh yes he did! He always does. There is no such thing as unanswered prayer – ever. We have looked at five possible answers; there are no others. We may not get what we asked for; we often won't. But we can be quite sure that God always hears our prayers; we can be equally sure that he deals with them. Our heavenly Father, unlike human fathers, is never too busy.

It is inconceivable that God, who is a loving Father, would ever ignore a request from one of his children. So God always responds when we pray; it is up to us to discern what the response is. Maybe God has something to teach us, or there is something we have to do. Perhaps our prayer was simply selfish; we were concerned with *our* wants and desires and not with God's will and purposes. Perhaps we were trying to use God as Superman instead of asking him to use us. Perhaps we were putting ourselves at the centre of our prayers instead of God.

One reason we have difficulty in recognizing God's answers to our prayers is that we expect the answer to come on our terms, not his. We send a message; if it is not complied with, it must have been ignored or refused. But prayer doesn't work like that. Because prayer is a spiritual exercise, the normal human rules of communication don't apply.

Sometimes we really do try to listen to what God has to say to us, but we have difficulty in discerning the answer, or relating it to the prayer. That is because we are not as expert as we should be at receiving the heavenly signals. It is something we hope to get better at as time passes, although there will always be things that we cannot understand in this life and are not meant to. Indeed, one measure of wisdom is the realization that our little store of knowledge shades off into a vast area of mystery. In the meantime we can have complete confidence that if we have prayed, God has heard.

Not only has he heard, but he has taken whatever action is for our highest good. He has no overloaded in-tray into which he puts items that he will get round to dealing with in due course. If we pray, God *always* responds.

Once we have grasped this fact, we can learn to recollect recent times of prayer and ask ourselves which of the five answers was relevant. All too often, we make prayer requests and then forget that we made them. Not only does that mean that we often fail to say thank you when the request was granted; it also means we fail to learn what God wants to teach us.

If the answer was 'No', have we realized why? If it

was 'Wait', have we resolved to be patient and trusting? If it was 'DIY', are we going to get on with it? And if it was 'MYOB', has that given us a new awareness of God's wisdom and sovereignty? If so, our prayers are becoming increasingly fruitful, which is surely as it should be.

Every time of prayer, then, should bring us a little closer to God. He knows everything about us, but we constantly need to learn more about him. As we get to understand him better, we will avoid making every time of prayer a sort of religious 'Jim'll fix it', and use it to ask God to direct our lives, refine our natures, increase our knowledge of his truth and purposes, and use his power to bring help and healing to those who need it.

Can you think of any four things more worthwhile than those?

Appendix 1

Biblical references not given in the text

Chapter 1

Elijah on Mount Sinai: 1 Kings 19.

The gift of tongues: principally 1 Corinthians 12 and 14, but there are other references in Acts.

Chapter 2

The man who asked for more faith: Mark 9:14–29.

Chapter 3

The prodigal son: Luke 15:11–32.

The psalmist describes himself as a worm: Psalm 22:6.

Abraham pleading for Sodom: Genesis 18:16–33.

Jonah's crossness: Jonah 4.

Elijah's sulks: 1 Kings 19:1–18.

Chapter 4

Jesus' nights of prayer: Luke 6:12.

Saul and Barnabas sent from Antioch as missionaries:

Acts 13:1–3.

Chapter 6

Peter's escape from prison: Acts 12:1–19.
God's giving contrasted with human fathers: Matthew 7:9–11.
Nahor's search for a wife for Isaac: Genesis 24:1–27.
Joseph interprets Pharaoh's dream: Genesis 41:16.
Bitter water in the desert: Exodus 15:22–25.
Hannah's prayer for a son: 1 Samuel 1.
Solomon's prayer for wisdom: 1 Kings 3:4–15.
Nehemiah's concern for Jerusalem: Nehemiah 1 – 2.
King Hezekiah prays for deliverance: 2 Kings 19:14–19.
Cornelius' prayer for guidance: Acts 10:30–33.
Paul's prayer for healing of Publius' father: Acts 28:8.
Peter's prayer brings Tabitha back to life: Acts 9:36–42.
Isaiah's comment about Judah not praying: Isaiah 65:1.
Elijah on Mount Carmel: 1 Kings 18:20–40.
Paul on duties to state authorities: Romans 13:1–7.

Chapter 7

Paul's 'thorn in the flesh': 2 Corinthians 12:7–10.
Paul's argument with Barnabas: Acts 15:39.
Paul's bad eyesight: Acts 9:1–9; Galatians 4:15; 6:11.
Paul's visit to Galatia: Acts 13:13; Galatians 4:13.
The prayer of Jesus in Gethsemane: Matthew 26:36–46; Mark 14:32–42; Luke 22:39–46.
Jesus' prediction of Peter's denial: Matthew 26:31–35; Mark 14:27–31; Luke 21:32–34; John 13:36–38.
Stephen's witness before the Council: Acts 7.

Chapter 8

Jesus' prayer for the unity of his followers: John 17:11, 21, 23.

Prayer for Christ's return: Revelation 22:20.

First-century expectation of Christ's return: 2 Peter 3.

Jesus' exhortation always to pray and never become discouraged: Luke 18:1–8; 11:5–8.

Paul's advice to be 'persistent in prayer': Colossians 4:2.

Chapter 9

The Great Commission: Matthew 28:19–20.

James on faith and actions: James 2:14–26.

Paul's prayer life: 1 Thessalonians 1:2 (and similar verses in other letters).

Jesus prays for us: John 17.

Chapter 11

Demon possession: Luke 4:31–37; 8:1–3, 26–39: 9:1, 37–43; 10:17–20. (There are other passages in Luke and similar passages elsewhere.)

Mugging on the Jerusalem–Jericho road: Luke 10:25–37.

Being controlled by the Spirit: Romans 8:1–17.

Paul's 'thorn in the flesh': 2 Corinthians 12:7–10.

Satanic attacks: 1 Peter 5:8.

Chapter 12

Elijah on Mount Carmel: 1 Kings 18:20–40.

Abraham on Mount Moriah: Genesis 22:1–14.

God created human beings like himself: Genesis 1:27.

Sickness not a punishment for sin: John 9:3.

Chapter 13

The disciples ask Jesus to teach them to pray: Luke 11:1.

God feeds the birds and clothes the wild flowers: Matthew 6:25–30.

Jesus declares that our Father in heaven knows our needs: Matthew 6:31–34.

Paul on his natural inclination to sin: Romans 7:14–25.

Paul on 'being put right with God': Romans 3:21–26 (and other passages).

Our being made perfect in heaven: 1 Corinthians 15:42–50.

Jesus' prayer that Peter's faith would not fail: Luke 22:32.

The high-priestly prayer of Jesus: John 17.

Paul's sufferings for the gospel: 2 Corinthians 11:16–29.

Chapter 14

God as a wise Father: Matthew 7:9–11.

Appendix 2

A paraphrased Lord's Prayer

(Tune: 'Annie's Song')

Our Father in heaven, Creator almighty,
We worship and praise you, your name we adore.
So bring in your kingdom, when all will obey you,
Return in your glory and reign evermore.

Your hand has provided, our food never faileth;
Please help us to trust you for other things too.
Our sins we confess, Lord; we bring them before you.
In mercy, forgive us, and cleanse and renew.

We too would forgive, Lord, all those who have
wronged us;
So help us to love them, seek only their good.
Protect us from evil, and save us from sinning;
Then when we are tempted, we'll do as we should.

All honour is yours, Lord, all power and all glory;
Your wisdom is perfect, your love is sublime.
Your truth is eternal, your power is unfailing;
Your name shall be reverenced, now and for all time.